WHEN THEY CHEAT

Recovering Power and Purpose in the Face of
Loss and Uncertainty

DW LONG, LCSW

For more information contact DW Long, LCSW at www.mcscoach.com

ISBN: 978-1-3999-0951-8

Library of Congress Cataloging-in-Publication Data is available.

10 9 8 7 6 5 4 3 2 1

First edition December 2021

Cover design by Krishna Mohan

Copy Editor: Emma Moylan

Dedication

For my extraordinary teacher Maria Curcio.

You taught me more about living life to the fullest than anyone else in this lifetime. Through our deep dives into Chopin, Bach, Schumann, and Schubert, you imparted wisdom that has resonated with me since the moment it was given. I lost my way a few times, but your presence, like a compass, always guided me back to the path. I love you.

Acknowledgments

Many thanks to the following people. If you are mentioned here, your support holds great and immeasurable value for me. Thank you to:

Graeme Strachan for being my partner in more ways than anyone ever has. Your insight is invaluable and I trust you with my whole being.

Kemi Nekvapil for reminding me to never forget that my and everyone's voice is worthy of being heard.

Jaema Hayes and **Andy Macon** for being the kind of friends everyone wants to have.

Maria and **Sandra Bowskill** for your steady, luminous presence and cosmically fabulous lightness of being.

Chris Schubert, my sister, for often opening the door to a learning moment and inviting me to walk through.

Nick Schubert for simply being the best nephew an uncle could ever ask for.

All of my **Clients** with whom I work in the psychotherapy and coaching arenas. It is always my privilege to hold space with you, learn from you, and for that I am truly grateful.

Emma Moylan for a fabulously precise copy edit on the body of this guidebook. Without you, this little book might have been a complete mess!

The thousands of **Social Media Followers** who show up like a stadium of cheerleaders, rooting for me in the most loving way every day. You guys rock my world!

Contents

Introduction

Times of crisis often bring on a reckoning for us humans. We lose a job, a loving friend or family member becomes ill and needs our support, or in alignment with this book, we discover that someone we have loved fully and wholeheartedly has done something that shatters our perception of who we are, or at least, who we think we are. Looking forward in this moment of crisis, we might find ourselves not knowing how to step into what is before us since our perception of who we are and what we thought was supposed to happen next has been splintered. Our *perception* of who we are might have been smashed to bits, but that perception is not and never will be who we really are. Our perception of who we are can be colored by our upbringing, the environment of our early development, adverse life experiences, the list goes on and on. Until we gain some clarity and develop the skills to observe this view for what it is, merely a perception of our experience, we will continue to create our own suffering—but more about that later.

It is in these times of crisis that we often find ourselves showing up in ways that are surprising, and we might even ask, "Where have I found the strength for this?" These moments can be truly luminous and exciting, since it is in these instants that we realize we are made of tougher stuff than we thought, hence the writing of this book. Yes, courageous reader, this book was born out of my own experience with this type of suffering—the painful revelation that my spouse had been unfaithful.

There are countless books floating around that guide people to try and "figure out" their sense and understanding of self. The laborious process of *figuring out* is not what this book is about. This book is about finding a clear path to being vulnerable while immersing ourselves in the curious exploration of who we really are. Now, when I say curious exploration, I mean finding a similar quality of curiosity about ourselves that is very much like that of a two-year-old who has been handed an object they have never seen before: Wondrous fascination ensues! I encourage you to embrace this type of magical curiosity as you make your way through this book. In truth, curiosity can only bring us closer to our *self*, and if we have decided to engage this curiosity while infusing it with the presence of Love, then we have set ourselves on the most magnificent journey of self-discovery we might have ever experienced. Most importantly, know that the pain we are exploring and the discomfort we are holding is just simply that—pain and discomfort, nothing more. I can hardly think of anything more empowering than that realization.

My greatest hope is that the insight and vulnerability I bring here along with the tools I present, some of which are my build on the brilliance of others, bring light to your path. This book was written at the start of my own experience with this subject matter so everything I bring here is from direct experience as a human being who has experienced this type of suffering as well as my experience as a therapist and coach. Wisdom from individuals such as Brené Brown, Joseph Campbell, Pema Chodron, Ram Dass, Dawna Markova, Kemi Nekvapil, Eckhart Tolle, Tara Brach, Daniel Seigel, Iyanla Vanzant, and Maria Nemeth, is brought here for you to integrate into your own experience.

You will notice that I have sometimes personified words/elements such as Truth, Clarity, Courage, Fear, Pain, Love and Grace in various parts of this book. Over the course of my lifespan, these elements have most often felt like entities who come into my vicinity possessing certain attributes - at least in my imagination. Sometimes these attributes are threatening and other times these presences feel like the arrival of a superhero ready to save the day. Courage arrives to battle with Fear while Grace brings along her friend Clarity to help me see more clearly where I stand on my path. My hope is that in using this device, you will engage your own imagination and connect with your internal resources in a novel and creative way.

By the time you finish reading this book, you will have tapped into the truth that you are a powerful being and hopefully you will begin to experience that power fully. When you rest in that power, your sense of purpose will become clear to you, whether you are discovering it for the first time or coming back in alignment with it.

Be gentle with yourself as you are reading along and striding into this expedition of courageous self-study. BE gentle.

Initial Shock and the Hero's Journey

*Our inner hero shows up
when we say "yes" to life.*

And here we are … together. You and I, dear reader, have had a terrible wrong perpetrated against us. Perhaps you came across this little book in the bookstore or airport or even went searching for it online. Right now, you might be in the throes of great suffering having discovered that your partner, spouse, lover, or whatever name you give to your significant other, has cheated on you. The one thing you thought was certain has now been inundated with the presence of uncertainty. Like being thrust into an unfamiliar landscape with insufficient tools to find your way home, the discovery of this rude truth might have you feeling devoid of resources and left with the hollow pang of shock.

Many of you reading these words have experienced this initial shock very recently or in the not-too-distant past. Rest easy in knowing that if you are on a search for resources, you have found them. So, take a breath and know that if all is not well in this moment, all will be well in the end.

Throughout this book, I talk about building one's capacity for *being with* all of the difficulties before us rather than running away from them, suppressing them or even worse, medicating them with negative behaviors such as rampant drug and alcohol use, overeating, and isolation. If you are wondering what you might do to steady the turbulence during this initial shock phase, ask yourself this question: What is the most loving and kind thing I can do for myself in this moment of suffering?

For some, this will not be the first question that arises. Some of us, as I have done in the past, will seek to stop the suffering, run away from the circumstances and try to live in a manner that blocks healing and keeps the pain festering away inside some deep recess. When faced with this sort of pain, many of us numb ourselves, avoid, tune out and do everything in our power to *not feel*. You might have heard or read somewhere that this type of coping never works. You may already believe this notion from the sidelines but have never fully stepped forward and stood nose to nose with your pain. Or, perhaps you have experienced the freedom that comes with embracing and leaning into the pain with an open and courageous heart. I was never very good at this leaning in thing … until I was. And that, dear reader, took a long time. So, be gentle with yourself and read on.

THIS LEANING IN IS GUTSY AND YES, YOU REALLY CAN do exactly what I am talking about here, whether you choose to believe me in this moment or not. Leaning in may mean that you muster the most courage you have ever mustered in your life and in the end, if you choose to take this mission, the payout is most certainly exquisite. The payout I speak of is an understanding of your true self and a mastery of your own mental operations. This mastery can afford you the ability to thrive in any situation. Although suffering is an integral part of life and pain can be experienced around any corner, thriving in the presence of pain and suffering is truly empowering. And that, courageous reader, is what this book is about.

Initial shock

It started with an earthquake. Asleep in my home in Knoxville, Tennessee, after spending three months in Italy, I found myself suddenly awake at 4:17 a.m. I checked the time and in my irritation for being awake so early, I found my mind wandering into an area I didn't want to traverse. At this uncivilized hour, I didn't know there had actually been an earthquake, a small one, 4.4 on the Richter scale, occurring just minutes before I found myself checking the time. With my sleep being disturbed and finding myself shifting from a drowsy fog to being wide awake, the unsettling notion of engaging in a confrontation with my spouse began to press on my brain, a sensation not unlike having a cast iron skillet resting on the top of my head—heavy, pitiless and fresh off the stove.

My intuition had been whispering to me for a long time that something was askew in my relation-

4

ship and although I didn't want to admit it, I knew that today was the day I was going to confront the truth—or so I thought. Funny how Truth is often denied the pride of place to stand in its fullness when wrapped in guilt and shame. Although I did not know that the truth would be held from me on this day, I set out to find it nevertheless. With much trepidation, I brought up the topic of extramarital affairs and the possibility that such a thing might be occurring in our relationship.

As it happened, Truth was held captive and I was met with a lie. Questioning myself and attempting to cut through the scrapple in my head, I began to pore through the layers of my anxiety, while finding myself overcome with the intense fear that my mental health was poor. I wondered, "Am I having paranoid delusions?" My mind pelted me with thoughts like, "Perhaps my anxiety has driven away my partner, so no wonder they have retreated." I tried to rationalize my way through what I thought was happening and what I found was blame and shame toward myself, not the clarity that would eventually shake me from this hard-bitten nightmare of destructive thoughts. Somehow through the fried mess that was my current mindset, my intuition kept singing to me. A quiet voice kept urging me to *stay the course, stay the course*. So, stay the course, I did. After taking a breath (or more like a hundred shallow and not at all mindful inhalations and exhalations with my anxiety raging), I found the welcome presence of clarity. A few days later, having found a few kernels of courage after rummaging around in the deep pockets of my brain and heart, I stepped forward with much more precision resting at the forefront of my being. I was clear as I set my intention to allow Truth to come forward. And this time, Truth met me face-to-face. Although painful to hear and very much to my surprise, Truth with its steel girded certainty brought far less suffering than the viscous uncertainty I had been wading neck-deep in when I had been questioning my sanity only days before.

In some deep pocket far back in the recesses of my being, I held the hope that my spouse would become angry or defiant while shouting at me that cheating had never happened. If this were true, I would be compelled to believe it and would begin walking the path to deconstructing my poor mental health. But this was not how the story was to unfold. I am forever grateful for Truth to be unveiled and stripped free of deception, even with the pain that was experienced immediately following the admission. Truth arrived naked and vulnerable yet more powerful and clear than any measure of deception could ever hope to sustain. Truth had been freed from the clutches of its former captor, my spouse. And as Truth always does, Truth prevailed.

Although relieved by the admission, a deep sense of loss accompanied by bristling uncertainty was the beginning of the mix of feelings that would inundate me in the coming days. While I steadied myself, I found I had greater clarity than I thought I would ever have imagined in a moment like this. As I packed my things to leave, I asked myself why I was so calm and why was it that I wasn't coming apart at the seams? Hours into the drive away from my spouse, the first seedlings of this book were beginning to sprout and I didn't even know there had been seeds planted in the first place. Most welcome was the presence of Grace, her arm around my shoulder to steady and soothe me. I knew that there was work to be done and I somehow knew this work had to begin with more self-exploration on my part. I knew that I had tools to survive this without coming apart at the seams … or did I?

. . .

A TINY MORSEL OF PERSONAL DISCLOSURE

Historically, when I was younger, my capacity for self-reflection in moments of deep distress, bad news, and so on had been either nonexistent or had run at barely a trickle. At one time in my life, I was hopelessly ill-equipped to deal with the "hard stuff." It is only during the past decade that I have through meditation practice, prayer and my desire to stay connected to something bigger than myself been able to find balance in moments like these, all practices for which I am truly grateful. For they, I have discovered, are the foundation from which I have been able to continue building my life and being a contribution, all the while staying connected to a sense of purpose. In the past, my sense of purpose and contribution were usually the first things to fly out the window during life's extreme challenges. But not now. Now, I am able to share this experience by writing this book and drawing upon the many wisdom traditions that have been accessible to me in recent years. My hope is that you, courageous reader, will not only find comfort in these passages but will find solid tools to keep you afloat during this difficult time.

FIRST STEPS

So, how do we take our first steps toward a

place where we can breathe and begin to look at our current situation, assess where we are in this moment and actually connect to our ability to thrive? What are the elements that afford us the aptitude to rebalance and find clarity in a time of uncertainty and bitter chaos? While reading this book, I will suggest to you that although you might read the chapters in the order they are presented here, your initial steps toward healing might occur in a different order. Although my experience required me to first be able to breathe and connect with my own inner light while holding the dark tenderly and with much love, you might decide that the first thing you need to do is seek support, which I talk about in chapter nine, "Shouting Out for Support." There is no exact formula for how to approach this process, so be gentle with yourself and read this book with an open mind and an open heart, while taking away what works for you. Ditch the rest and again, know that all is well and all will be well in the end. You may find yourself coming up with your own unique ideas and when you do, I encourage you to share those experiences, tools and innate skills with others who are in the throes of a similar experience.

. . .

NOT UNLIKE AN EARTHQUAKE, A SUDDEN SHIFT IN the dynamics of our current experience can be completely unexpected and most definitely unwelcome. In popular culture, we see tons of images and phrases that suggest we all should embrace the *life is a journey* paradigm. We read books about this principle alongside being bombarded by memes on social media that distill this notion down to its most basic and, I think sometimes, unhelpful reduction. We listen to self-help gurus and media personalities proclaim the benefits of embracing this idea. To be transparent, I fully embrace the life is a journey principle. However, it can be very easy to become frustrated when this simple idea is difficult to assimilate and integrate into our current experience.

THE PROBLEM? TO FLIPPANTLY OVERLAY A simplified version of what our heroic path is actually about keeps us from honoring the complexities, difficulties and the true learning curve needing our embrace in this moment. None of this is easy and if we try and make it so or pretend that it is, the process that is rigorous and meant to be fully honored ends up looking like some kind of spiritual bypass. The solution? Perhaps we hold the life is a journey principle in our minds and hearts while we gently and meticulously unpack all of the painful elements that are present in our current experience and hold them fully. This is a very mindful way of living since we are asking ourselves to be truly present to every component of what is currently happening, while not throwing a generalized blanket of warm and fuzzy over it. Yes, this practice requires us to engage in a kind of self-study and this self-study must be infused with curiosity, openness, acceptance and love. Sounds easy and pretty straightforward, doesn't it? As you embark on this journey, you might find this process flows with great ease. You might also discover that this will be the most difficult path you have ever traversed. To walk it is your choice and I imagine since you have read this far, you are willing to continue.

When we discover that parts of this journey are not straightforward, it is in this moment that we can begin the practice of fully acknowledging ourselves and the heroic journey we are currently navigating our way through. Acknowledging ourselves for being on this heroic journey is an absolute must! We must begin by honoring and bringing love to the self. In this moment, we are being called to carry ourselves lovingly through this experience by our truest self. When we are clear, we understand that no one else can do this for us.

Setting out on our own in this time of uncertainty is one element that makes this journey truly heroic. This path is ours and ours alone, hence, it's time to talk about the hero's journey and bring a perspective from someone who defined this journey with the utmost clarity.

HERO'S JOURNEY AND THE TRUE SELF

Joseph Campbell greatly influenced the way we view our human experience, most notably by helping to define archetypal features of the hero's journey. In his book *The Hero with a Thousand Faces*, Campbell explores the hero's journey by bringing insight from psychology and blending it with his vast understanding of comparative mythology. If you have ever seen a *Star Wars* film, then you have had a firsthand experience of his contribution to our understanding of what it means to be human and to be a hero. To be human and to be a hero are two concepts that cannot be divided in my opinion. All of us experience bliss and suffering, good times and bad times, and when we learn to hold all of it in the same breath, we are truly embracing the hero's journey. We are declaring that all of it simply *is* and by making this declaration, we empower ourselves to face anything that comes our way with the fullness of our being.

. . .

ONE PASSAGE FROM *THE HERO WITH A THOUSAND Faces* that I find impactful and pertinent to our journey together tells us that the hero is someone from whom something has been taken. The hero is then called to go on an extraordinary adventure to either recover something that has been lost or discover some life-giving potion that will change the course of the hero's path for the better. At the culmination of this adventure, the hero will return having won the battle with either themselves or the battle against a greater evil, bringing home the trophy of wisdom and experience.

SO, COURAGEOUS ONE, LET'S DECONSTRUCT THIS. On our hero's journey, something has definitely been taken from us: our current understanding of what we thought we knew, the outline we held in our minds and hearts about what our future might look like, our sense of certainty, the belief in ourselves and our worthiness, the list goes on and on. What do you think about this idea of the journey being a cycle where we, the hero, go into the world to face the adventure before us and return having grown and perhaps even found some mastery in our life experience? Might Mr. Campbell's ideas be pointing to the notion that despite the chaos and uncertainty that surrounds us in this dark moment, where we feel like we might have lost a sense of who we are, our adventure is all about returning to ourselves? Our truest self? That is my thinking since when I received the news that my spouse had been unfaithful, my sense of self was essentially obliterated. All of the negative questions regarding my worthiness and my being enough fell upon me like an avalanche: heavy, smothering and unrelenting.

THE GOOD NEWS HERE IS THAT OUR TRUEST SELF IS always with us. It is who we really are and cannot be separated from us. Our true self knows that the journey ahead of us is difficult, yet the true self refuses to shy away from the challenge. Our true self knows what we need in any given moment and all we need to do in this moment is learn to listen. If at one time in our lives we possessed the skill that enabled us to truly listen to our true self, then tuning in right now can be as simple as selecting a station on the radio. On the flip side, if we have questions or doubts about our ability to tune in, the journey here holds even more for us since rediscovery and reconnection with that self can feel all the more rewarding. When we have a true self experience, whether it is our first time or if we are realigning ourselves to tune back in, a sense of peace, empowerment and courage becomes the norm. Perhaps more importantly and even surprisingly, we often find access to strengths we didn't know we possessed. This is some good news!

READY TO SAY "YES" TO YOUR TRUE SELF?

2

Finding Courage

Connecting to our true self requires courage.
Without courage, we cannot manifest our heart's desires.

I imagine that courage is something that resides within us at all times. It is not something that we need to search for outside of ourselves, even though we often find inspiration from the courageous acts of others. Whether or not these acts occur through the stories of fictional characters or if they happen right before our eyes by the people we know in physical reality, courage is part of our inherent makeup, whether we believe it or not.

. . .

As we set out on this new journey alone, while seeking answers from within and without in our hope to reestablish a sense of certainty to move forward, it behooves us to recognize and acknowledge that we possess everything we need in order to make this journey and have it become a fulfilling and successful one.

As we stand here at the beginning of this path, most of us are probably faced with the accompanying fear that is inevitably present in situations like this one. Our minds begin dredging up countless negative thoughts, some of which are part of patterns we have grown used to throughout our life experience. There are even perhaps new and unwelcome fears arising that have stories all their own. There are stories we have never seen or heard before running rampant in our minds. If you are at all like me, those new stories are all the more frightening since they come from a place unknown, perfectly poised to dance arm in arm with uncertainty. In the background, there is some dreaded music playing that we can't either turn off or turn to a lower volume. Nightmarish …

.   .   .

One thing for which we can be certain is that Courage thrives in the presence of Fear. Courage is the kid who refuses to be bullied. With Fear riding shotgun, Courage is the voice that says, "you got this," even when all of the evidence points to the possibility that we don't "got this." In truth, there can be no courage without the presence of fear, period. So, how is it that we engage our courage in moments like this, alone and thrust onto a path we never asked to cross? There are lots of memes out there that tell us to embrace the fear. I don't really know anything about embracing the fear, but I do know that allowing Fear to be there while we continue moving forward courageously is a tried and true means of truly being with courage. Fear is then free to stand on the sidelines while we get on with it.

Fear attempts to halt us from being fully with our built-in capacity for courage and this is where setting our intention can come to play. In these moments, it is up to us to choose who we want to play with. Will we enjoy playing with Fear, who tells us that we are unworthy, ugly or that we lack courage? Or, will we invite Courage into our arena and be reminded that we are whole and complete, creative and resourceful and have everything we need to make it through this?

Yes, dear reader, this might sound oversimplified, way too easy and perhaps too good to be true. However, throughout the course of this book, we will look at many different ways to be connected to our best self. We will explore connection to that self by asking for support, by being in silence with ourselves and looking inward with a sense of space. Most importantly, we will study how to connect to our best self by being gentle. So, if you can, stay the course and read on.

A practical approach

When we are searching for ways to be more courageous, finding advice is as simple as typing a query into a search engine on the Internet. There are a ton of coaches and therapists providing practical knowledge surrounding harnessing our ability to tap into our courage. Much of what you might find on this search has very little mention of approaching this process in a gentle way. We find articles suggesting that we can change our thinking by manipulating our thoughts to ward off fear. Although cognitive approaches have somewhat of a proven track record, the aggressive and rather unyielding approach of manipulation seems harsh and unrelenting. We manipulate steel, chemical compounds and sometimes other people to get what we want. So, this begs the question for me, do we need to see our truest self as something that needs manipulation so that we achieve the outcome we so desire— finding courage? I don't think so.

Some authors boldly proclaim that preparing for the worst possible outcome is the way to go. I also find this unsettling since, as an anxious person myself, peering into the future and expecting the worst can only achieve two things: upping the ante on my anxiety, while thrusting me entirely out of the present moment. In truth, we are looking to tap into our courage right now—not sometime next week or next month and certainly not at the last minute when the worst does show up on our path. As far as many of us are concerned who are experiencing the pain surrounding the subject matter of this book, the worst is here and there is absolutely no time like the present.

So, what is this gentle path I am speaking of? As we explore many ways of holding our pain throughout the course of this book, the notion of simple, mindful observation of anything that plagues us, I am going to argue, is the most rapid path to healing we can take.

Imagine this: What would it be like for you to simply observe Fear as if it were an entity standing far on the other side of a large room from you? This entity is not attached to you in any way and it is far enough away in this moment to cause you no harm. You can see Fear clearly. Perhaps you can see how it is dressed, the expression on its face, the subtleties of its body language and while you rest in the knowing that in this moment it has no power over you, you simply observe it. I fully understand that this might be a difficult thing to imagine since most of us experience our fear internally. But as an exercise, a very mindful one, imagine being able to take on the scenario fully.

How might it feel? Is it possible that you would feel a sense of power knowing that you are safe? Would you stand in recognition of that fear and have a completely different experience if Fear were completely detached from you? This type of observation is in direct alignment with the kind of gentle observation I have begun speaking of here and we will continue to do this with many aspects of our experience throughout the entirety of this book.

Now, it's time to take a breath, a very gentle one, allow what you have read thus far to find a space to rest inside you and when you are ready, continue the journey through this book.

See you again soon.

3

Out of the Darkness

The greatest connection to our humanity comes when we willingly step into the place where fear resides and meet it with an open heart and an open mind.

W hat can be born out of a moment of darkness? We might jump to holding on to the idea that only pain and suffering are born out of darkness since it is our default response to believe so. This begs the question: What kind of light can be experienced in a moment of darkness? When we think about balancing dark and light in our lives, it can seem like an impossible trick to perform. As I reflect on my past, arising out of a dark night of the soul some years ago, came some of my most luminous contributions in this world today. For example, I went through several years of active addiction—alcoholism. I became dependent upon it after experiencing a very bleak time where I felt my contribution was valued at little to nothing. Being externally focused and believing that everything existing outside myself was a primary determinant for any level of happiness, I did no more than exist day-to-day in this limited way of being. At one point, I had no sense of direction and had absolutely no understanding of my purpose in this world. The trauma I experienced as a child had shown up in my later development and was a primary instigating factor for initiating a figurative failure to launch sequence. I had come to a stop and was perhaps even sliding backward. With the death of my mother, my biggest fan, I thought I had lost the only touchstone for my sense of worth. I was, to say the least, lost. Thanks to some loving support from my sister and a few others, I was able to connect with my true self and set the intention to be well. Iyanla Vanzant tells us that every painful experience that leaves us wounded needs a witness and I am grateful for the support I received, as difficult as it was to accept.

AFTER SOME TIME AND HAVING FOUND A RENEWED sense of wellness, the forward momentum toward well-being increased as I continued to seek support from therapists, others who found themselves recovered from their addiction and people in my life who wanted to see me thrive and be at my best. In the end, the clarity that I was afforded when I got sober allowed me to set in motion the mindset and *heartset* that I am currently living in—to be a loving contribution to the world.

I SAY MINDSET AND HEARTSET HERE BECAUSE I believe our greatest contribution comes when we find a balance between head and heart. Our heart guides us to the place where we want to be: a place where we feel good, appreciated and are able to recognize with clarity our purpose and contribution. The mind is there to help us critically think through our movement on the path before us and if we can maintain mindful clarity, we are able to make our way through difficult spots, barriers and anything that holds us back from being in flow— even those obstacles of our own creation. If you are at all like me, you might have become adept at creating lots of your own obstacles across the course of your lifespan. Ah, to be human ...

. . .

NOT LONG AFTER RESTING IN SOBRIETY, I BEGAN TO feel that my contribution was somehow focused in the area of being of service to other people and helping others in some way. At the time, I had no idea how that might look. So, I began volunteering in the detox center of a treatment facility where I was able to interact with people who were in the throes of active addiction, an experience I understood personally. These individuals were still experiencing delirium tremens, hallucinations and quite often the inability to string a thought together with any clarity. As I sat with these sparks of divinity, I saw myself over and over again. I spoke to people who were surrounded by other people in their everyday lives but felt intensely alone in the world. Individuals who had hopes and dreams only to have a car accident or an injury suffered on a worksite found themselves thrust into becoming addicted to substances, painkillers and the like. Either to dull the physical pain they were experiencing, or most notably, the emotional, psychological and spiritual emptiness they experienced, these individuals were undergoing intense suffering that they wanted to cease. Whether or not, courageous reader, you have experienced an addiction, you and I both know what it is like to feel pain, to suffer intensely and wish with every part of our being that it would simply stop.

. . .

BEING ABLE TO HOLD SPACE WITH THESE DARING individuals brought me a kind of clarity I had never experienced. Sitting with these men and women who were hell-bent on getting well so they could once again harness their best self, despite having the odds against them, triggered my calling to be a contribution in a new arena. After speaking to countless individuals who worked in mental health, I set about to go back to school and get a master's degree in clinical social work. During my practicum and immediately after my graduation, I worked with families experiencing acute imbalance, addicts seeking to find themselves again and people grasping for well-being. Now, in my private practices, I have met extraordinary individuals searching for their own way out of the dark in as many settings as one could imagine. The one thing that every single one of these individuals possess, including myself and you, courageous reader, is that the light they are seeking is already inside of them. Yes, there is no external light that we need to bring to our journey to make it easier—it truly resides within us. It may be dimmed in moments but it is always there and cannot be extinguished.

. . .

Now, years ago, if you had told me that everything I needed was already inside of me, I might have called "bullshit." I was of the belief that everything I needed was external to myself. Finding the right counselor to unlock and unpack those stowed away boxes full of unworthiness, loneliness and pain would surely bring me the happiness I sought. I thought that if I found the right person who could love me enough so that I might feel whole and complete, I would then have everything I needed to be fulfilled. It was all on the outside as far as I was concerned. I came to find out, that's where the real bullshit is. We are often taught that if we work hard enough, stay on the straight and narrow and do our best that our lives will be full and we will be happy. Bullshit. We are worthy simply by the very nature of us being here, as Oprah says, and when we get a glimpse of what it feels like to be no longer driven by anything external, we thrive. Nothing outside of ourselves needs to look pretty or be the perfect fit for us to truly find real, sustainable happiness. Upon reflection while writing these words, the realization that I had everything I needed to begin with is probably the one thing for which I am most grateful.

Pain

You might be feeling intense pain right now, a pain that is directly associated with the sense of loss and disempowerment you feel now that you have discovered someone you love has betrayed you. Believe it or not, this pain is not at all unlike the pain the addicted individuals I spoke of earlier were feeling in their darkest moments. I know this to be true because I have experienced both. When I realized that the love I held for someone was not highly valued by them, darkness descended upon me and its arrival buried me under a suffocating heft of pain. Unlike many other times in my life where I was looking to escape the pain, this time, I was able to hold it and perhaps even lean into it. In fact, setting our intention to lean into the pain and our sense of loss and uncertainty in moments like these actually means that we have connected to and asserted our power. We decide how much to hold, how hard to lean into the suffering and when all is said and done, the darkness we dread in moments like this can become not only bearable but even welcome. It is in this contrast that we are able to see and experience our true self—our best self. And when we are able to truly step aside and view how we are showing up in moments where darkness is ever-present, this simple act brings us a kind of mindful clarity. This clarity comes from choosing to be the witness to this experience rather than have the experience overtake us. A dose of curiosity, openness, acceptance and love can mean the difference between being swallowed by the darkness or picking up the light we all possess and moving forward with ever gaining momentum.

So, HOW DO WE TAKE THOSE FIRST STEPS ON A DARK or perhaps dimly lit path and bring our own light so that Clarity becomes a constant companion and well-being is ever-present? Earlier, I recounted how my path became lit with the notion of service and contribution. I got outside of myself and decided to take the loving energy I had and be present to others. So, I started asking the question, "What am I here to do today?" It is a question I ask of myself most every day and is always asked with an open heart and no need for an answer since every time I ask, the answer comes in some way, shape or form anyway. Every time.

As WE CONTINUE TO GET OUTSIDE OF OURSELVES and examine how to navigate the darkness that has settled around us temporarily, let's examine a simple process designed to help us observe our experience with some distance. For now, it is what we are here to do so, take your time with these next steps and trust your own aptitude for self-discovery.

RAIN

One of the first things we must do in moments of darkness before we begin to contemplate our exit strategy is to learn how to hold the pain and suffering that is present without running away. Yes, I said hold the pain and suffering. Again, this is about leaning into and being with the one thing we want to go away. If we can find a way to allow the presence of pain to simply be there without judging it or trying to fix it and perhaps not even trying to figure it out, what might this space provide us with regard to our capacity to heal?

RAIN IS A POWERFUL TOOL THAT CAN BE TRULY transformative, and if you have never heard of this acronym, read on—it really can help you look back with more ease and create more space for Grace to be present. RAIN can help us to introduce and increase the flow of self-compassion. While observing and applying the RAIN process to our experience, we might begin to understand that it is our own vulnerability in these moments that brings us closer to our truest self. In any dark moments in our lives and especially the moments being discussed in this book, some of us find ourselves in a tug-of-war on the inside. We fight with the feeling to be self-destructive while another force says to us that this is the time we should be taking the most precious care of ourselves—an uncomfortable place to be, for sure.

RAIN WAS BROUGHT TO US FROM THE FABULOUS mind of Michelle McDonald, a mindfulness teacher with decades of experience teaching vipassana meditation. It has been integrated into mindfulness teachings and practices for some time. Tara Brach, another presence on this earth for whom I have great admiration and the author of *True Refuge* and *Radical Acceptance*, speaks often of this practice. Through her contribution, RAIN has become a part of mainstream consciousness in various schools of thought associated with mindfulness and its application.

BRACH SAYS THAT RAIN CAN HELP US GET OUT OF the cycle of habitual creation of our own suffering. She beautifully discusses how this practice can help clear a path to a deeper sense of calm, which can then clear the way to a greater sense of openness to our experience in the present moment; being in the present moment is what we are talking about, right? When we are in the throes of a painful experience, being adept at shifting our attention and being able to *observe* our experience rather than be inundated by it is pretty much a superpower that can be developed by anyone. If being able to develop that superpower includes me, courageous reader, then it includes you too.

So, this is what RAIN looks like for me:

- R – Recognize what is happening
- A – Allow and accept
- I – Investigate inner experience with kindness
- N – Non-identification.

RECOGNIZE

In order to recognize what is happening, we must mindfully turn our attention to our thoughts, feelings and body sensations directly associated with the painful experience we are currently having. Our practice in this moment is to tune into our inner life. We might notice immediately that we are anxious and in doing so, fail to notice how our body is tightening, how we have butterflies in our stomach or any other uncomfortable sensations that might arise. At the onset of distressing emotions, one of the first things many of us lose is awareness of our breath. My breath tells me everything about where I am emotionally, psychologically and even spiritually. When we intentionally notice our breath, we connect to a clear signpost that is telling us how we are doing. As we direct our attention in this way, we discover that it is in this tuning in that we create space for observing thoughts and feelings rather than being overcome by the initial ensuing emotions. In this step, we are not here to fix, do, or figure out anything—we are simply observing.

You might be thinking, "How the hell am I supposed to calm down enough to simply observe my thoughts and feelings in this moment?" This is where mindful attention to the breath plays an important role, and if you are having trouble getting in touch with your breath as you begin this practice, find a good YouTube video on mindful breath and follow along. Or, read an article, download an app, find a book or even better, locate a practitioner and teacher of mindfulness and take a class. In essence, simply noticing the breath can bring you a wealth of information about yourself in the current moment. If you can connect to your capacity for mindful observation by simply noticing the breath without judgment, you will have engaged an innate superpower. Remember, be gentle always.

ALLOW/ACCEPT

Perhaps the original second step in RAIN was to allow. Throughout my study to become a mindfulness practitioner and teacher, I have come across presenting the notion of acceptance in this second step combined with the premise of allowing. So, in honoring both ideas, I like to pair allow and accept together. It is a good mix for me and for the individuals working with me and facilitates access to the mindset and heartset we are seeking here.

WHAT ARE WE ATTEMPTING TO DO WHEN WE SET our intention to simply allow whatever is going on inside of us to simply be there? One thing is true in this situation: We do not have to like what is happening in this moment in order to engage our ability to allow it to simply be what it is. By allowing everything to be as it is, we are laying the ground for facilitating a conscious decision about how we are observing our feelings instead of setting ourselves up to react negatively and mindlessly. This is a practice we must return to again and again since our default system will want to fight back and return to being reactive or worse, push away the pain. You might discover yourself saying, "Why am I being asked to allow this deeply painful experience to be here? The last thing I want to do is welcome more suffering!" And this, courageous reader, is where the real magic lies in practicing allowance. When we make the decision to allow something, that humble act possesses in its essence, kindness. If our current worldview is one where we see no kindness surrounding us, then why not create it for ourselves by drawing on the light that resides within us, as I mentioned before?

In blending acceptance with the practice of allowing, the two become partners in bringing us greater ease. For me, acceptance means that I am not only allowing something to be as it is but, in this allowance, I am removing judgment by accepting it fully. Perhaps this sounds like a simple act. I am not at all ashamed to disclose that in the beginning, when I first began practicing this feature of mindfulness, non-judgment was my greatest hurdle. I thought that if I accepted anything fully while also allowing it, it meant that I had lost control. At the time, I thought that control was the way for me to create any kind of balance or happiness. Line everything up, put it in order where I can see it and make sure nothing is askew. Only then will I feel happy … WRONG! I soon discovered that seeking to control everything created more suffering, while amplifying the feeling that things are out of place. As I stuck to this premise, I never discovered balance or happiness. Ever. Control was my modus operandi for much of my life, so again, practicing allowing and accepting was a tough one for me, to say the least.

BEING GENTLE WITH YOURSELF WILL SERVE YOU WELL in these moments. If you find you are in a mindset where these practices just aren't cutting it for the day, allow yourself to put them aside and accept the fact that today is just not a good day for trying this on. You might see now that by doing this activity, you are actually engaging the practices of allowance and acceptance anyway so, give yourself a break and be gentle.

INVESTIGATE

Here is where curiosity plays one of its greatest roles. In the next chapter, we explore curiosity in greater depth, but for now, let's just imagine investigating what is going on here with the mind of a two-year-old: playful, filled with wonder and perhaps even a little courage. Remember the first time you picked up a bug on your own? I do. It was one of those little roly-poly bugs called a wood louse and I must have played with that poor thing for an hour before I finally let it go. Perhaps we can engage our curiosity in a way that is not unlike that of a scientist on the verge of discovering something new. This is the type of investigation we want to do here. Curiosity about our feelings and emotions in these moments can provide us with the experience of creating some distance. Not unlike a child picking up that first bug, what happens if we are able to infuse this investigation with a sense of wonder and detachment? Like a scientist, can we put all of this under a figurative microscope and investigate it like it is something we have just discovered: unnamed, strange and something we would like to learn more about? Investigating with this sense of detachment and lightness of being means that we will stay away from the creation of more suffering. All of this was very difficult for me in the beginning and I really have to say here that if I can do it, you can do it. So, begin gently investigating what you are holding. I will state it again … begin gently.

· · ·

Non-identification

This is really your end result, what you are looking for. Non-identification means that we are able to see that the thoughts and feelings we are having in this moment are not who we really are. Yes, we are feeling and thinking them, but they are not the essence of our truest self. Our truest self is bigger than these things. Our true self possesses the innate capacity to observe all of this mindfully with some distance and that is what we are seeking to engage here. Engaging our true self means that we have the ability to observe everything that happens outside of us and all of the thoughts and feelings that come along with those experiences with a sense of detachment. As I mentioned before, this type of engagement can lead us to the realization that we are bigger than these things and that these things do not have to drive us to behaviors that create more suffering. For me, non-identification is the most mindful of qualities since we are deciding to empower ourselves by stepping away from the suffering, observing it with curiosity and love while simply letting it be what it is. We can sit in the knowing that the thoughts will pass, the feelings will recede and that we will have created space for the presence of Grace. It is marvelously fulfilling to have the experience of diminished suffering knowing that we have tapped into who we really are and set our intention to understand that we are not our thoughts and feelings. Intrusive thoughts and the accompanying feelings are fluid and fleeting. The end result of non-identification here is that we have a greater understanding of our self by creating distance in our observation. If that isn't empowering, I don't know what is.

So, COURAGEOUS READER, IF YOU ARE TAKING THESE first steps out of the dark, hoping that the light arrives very soon, are you willing to see what might happen if you create your own version of these practices? For some of you courageous souls, the answer will be "YES!" And if your answer is "no," there is no judgment for you here. I probably spent 75 percent of my life not even being aware of these practices and when they were introduced to me, I rejected them in the beginning. So, if that is your fight at the moment, what do you think I might tell you to do here? If your answer is to be gentle, then you are way ahead of where I was when these principles were first introduced to me.

BE GENTLE.

4

Sitting with Anger

Nobody will give us a harder time than ourselves.

Y ou might be thinking that the quote at the beginning of this chapter is probably not the most obvious one to place here, right? We are here to explore our anger that is directly related to what someone has "done to us." Or are we? You might also be thinking that the last thing you want to do right now is take any accountability for the suffering you currently feel. The absolute truth is that we are here to explore our anger and we are also here to explore how we take responsibility for everything in our experience—including our anger. If I have lost you here, take a breath and try reading on. If you simply can't in this moment, put the book down and come back when you are ready. I know that shortly after my discovery surrounding the premise of this book, I might have read the beginning of this chapter and needed to put the book down. I probably would have done so with a sneer and some off-the-cuff negative comment while walking away from it. After having chucked it onto a random pile of books waiting to be read that I would probably not get to anytime soon, who knows when I might have picked it up again? Some personal disclosure: The cynic rises often in me and has always been a side of my personality that poses challenges, to say the least. So, be gentle with yourself and take as much time as you need to come back, or continue onward.

IF YOU AGREE WITH ME THAT THE JOURNEY WE HAVE been thrust into is most definitely a heroic one, this might be the time to consider what type of environment or world we want to create for ourselves as we move forward down this path. We spend a lot of time in this book exploring the ins and outs of suffering together, and while we investigate the idea of sitting with anger, I really must say that this will have to be an area where we bring the most unconditional love to ourselves. This is the time to be the gentlest toward our self, believe it or not.

. . .

As we sit with anger, there are probably some things we need to consider. Are we going to add to the aggression we might feel toward our cheating spouse? Are we going to attend to the anger in a way that it becomes larger and overwhelms us? And if this antagonism is the way of being that we choose, when is our healing going to actually begin? I will argue that healing will not begin until we shrug off this way of being. I don't know about you, courageous reader, but for me, I find that when I fight with my resentment and anger in an attempt to overpower or destroy it, I find no clear space for healing.

Pema Chodron speaks in a richly fluid way to the notion of sitting with anger. In her teachings, she asks us to find the most tender and forgiving way of being toward ourselves in moments where anger rises up and threatens to strangle us. She suggests that instead of being harsh with ourselves, we should do the opposite. When we realize that we are creating our own suffering while in the throes of anger and have followed that predictable chain reaction that leads us to a place of bitterness and pain, this is the moment and the time to find gentle and ardent compassion for ourselves rather than the harshness we are habitually prone to bring.

· · ·

THIS BRINGS UP MANY QUESTIONS. IF OUR awareness brings us the capacity to pause instead of self-shaming or being hypercritical, what might happen if we are able to simply sit and feel the anger? What might happen for us when we allow the accompanying feelings like rage, pain, guilt and shame to just be there? What incalculable miracles might become possible when we humbly sit with anger, do nothing to it and mindfully put aside our desire to figure it out and most certainly negate any attempt to fix it? Pema Chodron asks us to simply allow anger to be what it is without escalation or attempt the inverse of that by trying to suppress it. If we can achieve this, we are in this moment choosing courageously to simply be with the anger —no small feat, for sure.

AS WE REFLECT ON WHAT KIND OF SPACE WE ARE creating for our next step toward healing, what do you think about this idea of simply sitting with your anger and doing nothing? I have to say that when this was first posed to me many years ago, the polarity of it felt so radically different than my way of being up until then that I rejected it full stop. My tendency was to strategize how to sort it out as soon as possible so that the suffering would end and I could get on with being "happy." Yes, happy is in quotes here since I actually had no idea what happiness truly was at this time, but I digress. It took me a while to figure out that my "strategy" was as built from the underpinnings of my ego, with these underpinnings being made from matchsticks: thin matchsticks with nary enough to fully support my so-called strategy. As it came to pass, with time and some good counsel from a very patient therapist, I began to realize that my habitual responses were not serving me. I was often easily thrust into an upward spiral of white-hot anger completely fueled by my own negative thoughts. Eventually, I decided that this was not the way I wanted to live. So, in a moment of resignation, hands thrown up with a dash of willingness present, I began to sit with the difficult feelings and emotions without doing anything to them, without trying to figure them out and above all, without trying to fix them. To this day, it is a practice I continue to utilize and I will say upon reflection that the baby steps I started with, although laden with some trepidation and a complete lack of understanding of what I was actually up to, it is these baby steps that I am forever grateful for.

. . .

How will this process start for you? Will you take time right now after reading this chapter to sit quietly and accept your anger for simply what it is —anger, nothing more? Perhaps you will decide that today is not the day for this excursion but will set your intention for a time that feels right for you. You might even have an experience similar to mine where you reject this idea completely and put the book aside.

Did you know that whatever you decide, your decision is the perfect decision for you? If today, next week or next month is not the time for you to begin sitting with your anger in the gentle way I am describing, understand this: There is nothing wrong with you or your process. You absolutely do not have to do the thing I am suggesting here for you to continue to be whole and complete—you are those things already, as I have said before. I will remind you that you have your own answers and the fact that you are taking time to read this book suggests that you are seeking to attend to the answers that you already possess. You might have hoped this book contains the solutions you need, but the truth is that the answers and solutions I bring here are universal by their very nature. I am simply bringing teachings here from many sources, both ancient and modern.

THE PRACTICE OF SITTING WITH, LEANING INTO, truly being with anger or any other uncomfortable emotion rather than avoiding it or suppressing it is present in more wisdom traditions than one can count, from ancient traditions both spiritual and philosophical to techniques utilized in modern psychology.

SO, WHEN YOUR INNER CYNIC RECEDES INTO THE background of your mind and you experience a moment of open curiosity, why not, just for experimental purposes, give this idea a go? Ask yourself if you have anything to lose. The truth is that if you do not step into the space of acceptance being created here, endeavor to attempt the practice of gently sitting with anger, you will never know the possible outcome. You will never know if this practice might bring you the ease you seek in this moment or be one of the first steps toward the healing you so desire.

. . .

So, ARE YOU FEELING CURIOUS? MORE importantly, is willingness present in this moment and overpowering the inner cynic?

I HOPE SO.

5

Looking Back

*Every moment is distinct in its quality
and cannot be repeated.
If we are awake enough, each moment can be learned from.*

Turning our minds and hearts toward the past with curiosity, openness, acceptance and love is probably one of the most powerful things we can do when reviewing what we've experienced. This practice can help us to see our past in the miraculous way the quote at the start of this chapter speaks to. This quality of observation can allow us to witness and hold all we have been through while allowing ourselves to feel everything that goes with examining this landscape. The distressing, uncomfortable and often unwelcome feelings can somehow be more bearable. For instance, setting up an agreement with your *self* that it is perfectly OK to have all of these feelings while creating the space internally to allow all of it to simply be there means that you are in charge. Nothing is happening by happenstance when setting your intention in this way. You get to decide how much of it you are willing to lean into and from there, in your own time, you can assimilate, process, deconstruct, or even figuratively chew on what it is you have chosen to wrestle with in the moment. I use the word "wrestle" here because my own experience in this arena often felt like I was wrestling to the death: wrestling with the pain, anger and sometimes resentment I was feeling. Wrestling and chewing … not very gentle words since, for me, they elicit images of fighting, pushing and tearing into something like the pain, but that was part of my experience at the beginning of this journey. For sure, this experience is not unlike hanging on for dear life to the back of a bucking bronco: It's not comfortable, you are gripping with every bit of strength you have while trying to figure out how in the hell you are going to avoid breaking your neck! However, I and countless others have discovered that fighting with pain and wrestling with resentment are futile investments since these actions stop us from being in flow. And when we are in flow, ease comes to any situation, no matter how dreadful, arduous or painful.

Dr. Daniel Siegel, who is one of my greatest heroes alive on this planet, created an acronym that penetrates the truth to a way of being that can bring ease when we are looking back. I have found this tool to be invaluable in my own experience and the experiences of the courageous individuals I serve as both a therapist and coach.

COAL

Curiosity
Openness
Acceptance
Love

Dr. Seigel speaks to how embracing these principles can bring us to a place of greater self-compassion. The quality of being gentle with ourselves while having compassion for ourselves can make any painful process more bearable, enhancing our sense of presence, which in the end allows us to attend to the hard stuff mindfully. We will look at some aspects of mindfulness throughout this book but for now, let's explore Dr. Siegel's acronym, COAL.

CURIOSITY

What does it mean to be curious? Oftentimes, the further into adulthood we travel, we find our curiosity might be tainted by a bit of cynicism and I am certainly guilty of this, as I have mentioned before. It is very easy to allow our curiosity to become analytical, results-driven and devoid of any playfulness. Even mild curiosity will serve us far better than the tiniest dose of cynicism. Imagine a two-year-old. He or she has but two years of life in this wondrous and sometimes precarious world. One of the most joyous, hilarious and fascinating events to witness is to hand said two-year-old an object he or she has never seen before. Wondrous curiosity ensues—curiosity that is so encompassing it seems to be a full-body experience for the child at hand. Checking out every curve, bend, color, smell and even sometimes taste becomes the one and only focus in that child's world. He or she is truly, I will say, acutely present. Our inborn aptitude for presence and being mindful can diminish as we age with all of the distractions available to us in this fast-paced and high-stress society. We are looking to recapture that sensation here. So, find yourself a two-year-old and hand them a small engine carburetor. I guarantee you will be delighted and so will they!

Can you look at your past and hold parts of it with the curiosity we are exploring here? Are you able to find a way to be playful when looking at the dark and difficult parts, to lovingly and with a sense of wonder explore what you have set out to explore? My answer to that question would be, "yes, you can!" You may feel a sense of pause or even disbelief when you read these words. Well, courageous reader, if there is any one thing I am right about in this book, it is the truth that any person laying eyes on this page, in this moment, has the capacity to do what I am talking about—the ability to allow curiosity to be present when unpacking everything from the past. Reminder: Not all of the past was dark or sharp-edged. There were luminous moments as well and although it might be difficult to find those points of light right now, remember why you are here. You are here to gain forward momentum in the aftermath of a cheater. You are here to get back in gear to thrive and be the master of your life. It's time for a little openness to accompany the curiosity.

OPENNESS

How might we approach our path in this moment of darkness with a sense of openness? For some, this might seem like an impossible feat. You might ask questions like, "How could I possibly be open when I have been harmed so greatly?" or "Isn't openness the last thing I need since I will be laid bare and vulnerable?" Many readers might know of the acclaimed social worker and researcher, Brené Brown. Her contribution to the world has been remarkable. Her research on vulnerability and shame brought to light that vulnerability is a way to connect not only with ourselves on a much deeper level but also affords us greater connection to others.

So, OPENNESS AND VULNERABILITY, HUH? IT MIGHT sound great in theory but for many, the idea of vulnerability, especially in moments such as these, seems out of the question. Let me tell you this from my own experience. Dr. Brown is 100 percent right. I could write page after page proclaiming the positive attributes of connecting to my own vulnerability. All I will say is this: In a moment when it seemed that all was lost, the life I had prepared for, the future I had anticipated that was now no longer going happen the way I had planned, staring into that seeming abyss before me, I made the mindful and intentional decision to allow myself to feel it all —free from judgment. Most importantly, I allowed myself to continue to be vulnerable. I lovingly decided to *be with* the pain, lean into the fear and sense of loss and most importantly, be gentle with myself. If a moment arose that I felt that could not hold any of it, I remembered the contract I made with myself—to be gentle. There were many of these moments and in my attempt to always be gentle, openness was present. We cannot be gentle with ourselves without the quality of openness being present as well.

ACCEPTANCE

I have been greatly inspired by the work and contribution of Tara Brach, author of *Radical Acceptance* and *True Refuge*. The notion that the practice of acceptance can help clear the pathway to healing and allow us to create space for mindfully observing whatever it is we have chosen to observe holds a deep resonance for me. Mindful observation is the key here. If we want to face all of those feelings that accompany the hard stuff, to do this wisely and successfully, we must truly be acutely mindful and resting in the present moment. A therapist might call those feelings and the content associated with them distressing affective material. I have used those words many times in my work but let's get away from the cold, clinical observation of what is truly going on. Let's just call it what it is—painful shit. My initial thoughts upon discovering that my spouse had been unfaithful were something along the lines of, "This is some fucked up bullshit that I didn't ask for!" If I were to take that one simple phrase and spin it into a long and filthy, tattered piece of mental fabric, then more suffering would wrap my entire life experience in distress and worry. Upon speaking those words either out loud or thinking them in my mind, I noticed that my feelings, my affective state and my gut didn't feel good. In the end, I began to understand that suffering would remain for as long as I entertained those thoughts and here is where the practice of acceptance comes in.

WE MUST COURAGEOUSLY ASK OURSELVES IF WE CAN accept fully and wholeheartedly that we are having these feelings. Ask yourself the question, "Am I able to be gentle with myself and practice non-judgment when these feelings are coursing through my entire being?" Sit with that for a second and know that these are important and challenging questions. If your answer to these is a resounding "no," then know that all is well and that you are not alone. In the beginning of my self-study, it took a very long time for me to be able to answer these types of questions with the "yes" we are looking for here.

IF NOT EVERYONE, MOST PEOPLE HAVE HAD THE experience of not being able to come to grips with the emotions and feelings they are experiencing at one time or another. For at least a couple of days after discovering my spouse had been cheating, my answer to these questions would not have been a resounding "yes." My inner *kumbaya* was nonexistent and I felt barren and devoid of any useful insight. Notably, because I have for a number of years practiced the elements of curiosity, openness, acceptance and love being discussed in this chapter, I noticed a yearning coming from inside asking me to reconnect with these principles while in the throes of almost debilitating emotional and psychological anguish. In allowing feelings, thoughts and the status quo to simply be, my suffering was diminished and my ability to be in the present moment was enhanced. This book could not have been written without my finding some modicum of acceptance for what was happening and what had already happened.

I HAVE INTRODUCED THE PRACTICE OF ACCEPTANCE to clients both in the therapy and coaching arenas and have experienced overwhelming gratitude from these courageous individuals for introducing them to the concept and the practice. Very much like me, many of these individuals did not want to insert this practice into their daily experience. Until they did. What has been reported to me is that, upon practicing acceptance, indescribably marvelous and transformative energies ensue, providing each individual with some sense of the light being on its way. And when we have this experience, we are able to remember that the light always returns—always.

Love

What can we say about love? Love is ever-present in our lives even when we cannot sense it. There is always someone out there who holds us in their heart. There are countless individuals with whom we have connected in a loving way on our path. A kind word to a stranger, a family member or friend we have held space for in a moment of suffering, a client with whom we have established a strong rapport and connection, all of these examples are indicative of the presence of love. Love is everywhere.

IF LOVE IS PRESENT EVERYWHERE, THEN WHERE DO we find it in moments where its presence seems imperceptible? It can be hard to feel love for and be loving toward ourselves in the midst of a breakup. It can be challenging to do even the simplest, loving things for ourselves in moments of loss and despair. Did you know that making your toast in the morning exactly the way you like it is a loving action? Did you know that doing this one simple act, making toast just the way you like it, is a way that your true self is saying, "I love you."

I CAN PICTURE SOME OF YOUR FACES RIGHT NOW. Smirking, rolling your eyes, mind shutting down, choosing to remove your presence from this experience and attend to something else. I talk about cynicism in the chapter, "True Self: Who Do You Think You Are." Be sure and read those passages about cynicism if your inner cynic has come into play. In a nutshell, cynicism never truly serves us and is a barrier to forward momentum, so if you are having the experience of not wanting to be curious, open, and accepting right now, it might be time to close this book and open it another time. It's all good since where you are right now is simply where you are in this process. Give yourself some space. Go for a walk, say a prayer, eat your favorite meal, cuddle with your favorite pet or do absolutely nothing. Simply give yourself some space.

FOR SOME OF YOU, FAR OFF IN THE DISTANCE, AS you read these words, you might notice a calling from somewhere inside of you saying, "listen!" It might be a whisper or it might be resounding loudly in your head and heart. Now and as always, your sense of presence will serve you, so trust yourself and go on to the next thing. If you are departing for the moment, see you later.

IF YOU HAVE CONTINUED READING OR HAVE PICKED up from where you left off at another time, let's start with an idea from a beloved teacher. The highly revered spiritual teacher Ram Dass reminds us that we never have to do anything to be loved. We are loved simply by the very nature of us exist-ing. Anything that we think detracts from that love is a symptom of monkey mind not based in any truth. For some, the notion that there is an immeasurable presence of love combined with the truth that it is all around us and is always accessible is not an easy concept to lean into, especially in moments when our entire notion of love has been challenged.

WE MIGHT FIND OURSELVES ASKING QUESTIONS regarding how it could be possible that Love is ever-present when the one person we have loved fully has seemingly taken Love away from us. We might begin to wrestle with our resentment and anger and what we sometimes find is that the longer we stay in this wrestling match, the farther away Love seems to be. We begin to feel bad, we have a pit in our stomach and as we continue to wrestle, we might notice physical changes, discomforts and signs that the suffering we are feeling, part of it anyway, is of our own creation. When we make the decision to set our intention to welcome and allow space for love to be present at all costs, we create room for healing, not only healing for our psychological, physical and emotional self but for our truest self, who we really are, love incarnate. We *are* love and since we are here, Love will always be here as well. Get it? Pretty simple really, even though it took me most of my life to figure this out.

· · ·

So, COURAGEOUS READER, WHEN LOOKING AT THE past, bring *all* of you. Most importantly, bring the love—it is what you are made of anyway. Practice acceptance where you can and forgive yourself for the places you can't. Stay open whenever possible and never forget to stay curious about yourself.

SEE YOU IN THE NEXT CHAPTER.

6

Wrestling with Pain

Pain is simply a part of our experience, nothing more.
We can fight it and suffer
or we can allow it to be what it is and thrive.

There are times on our life path when our sensitive, human selves will default to running away from pain by self-medicating, ignoring, or even flat out refusing to acknowledge any of the uncomfortable aspects of our current experience. The words at the beginning of this chapter hit the mark for me with its simple clarity about how this type of suffering is merely a part of the fabric of our experience—nothing more. If we practice acceptance here, what might shift us away from suffering and set us back onto the path to thriving?

WE KNOW THAT PAIN CAN LEAVE US FEELING groundless, with its unwelcome presence most often being rigid and unrelenting. I can assuredly say that pushing away Pain and avoiding it never serves us. Ever. If we try and do that, Pain simply waits in the corner, quietly searching for a way back into our experience, especially when we attempt to stifle it or send it away. Pain says, "I will be honored and until I am, I am not going anywhere." So, Pain follows us around, mumbling something that we don't want to hear, ever-present in the background noise of our lives until we turn around to face it and to give it the one thing it wants, to be acknowledged. Eckhart Tolle reminds us that whatever we fight, we strengthen, and what we resist perseveres. Rarely has there ever been a statement ringing with the clarity of truth like this one.

PRESENTED WITH THIS NOTION BY MY THERAPIST AT the beginning of the deepest suffering I had experienced to date, I became angry and commented that her job was to help me *eliminate* the pain, not lean into it. In fact, I got downright defiant about it. For the first time in my life, I was being asked to stand in front of my pain, look it in the eye and start a conversation—not at all what I had signed up for, or so I thought. What I discovered was learning how to truly be with Pain is one of the greatest gifts I have ever received.

If your experience is at all similar to mine, then you might be facing a moment of disappointment while reading this passage as we are not going to be looking at the elimination of pain. We are taking quite a different course of action. We are here on this hero's journey asking ourselves to cozy up to our uncertainty and wrestle with our pain full on. After all you have been through, you might be feeling a sense of desolation while trying to hold yourself together, wishing with all your might that the pain would stop. It is in this moment that we must remind ourselves that countless souls have had this experience and as we become more awake to this notion, of shared experience, we can begin to understand that this is one of those "rubber hits the road" moments. It's time to gear up, put our heads down and ride, am I right?

. . .

IN HER BOOK *COMFORTABLE WITH UNCERTAINTY*, Pema Chodron reminds us that during challenging times, it serves us to remind ourselves that the emotional difficulties we are experiencing are an indication that our comfort level has been disturbed. Not unlike being knocked off of our feet, we can choose to fight the discomfort or tune into it. When we choose to be with this discomfort in an open and vulnerable way, we are remembering that we are choosing to thrive in this lifetime rather than succumb to the struggle we are experiencing. This is once again a reflection of our heroic journey where we are being asked to do something extraordinary, to lean into the pain we are feeling with the fullness of our being.

LET ME SHARE THIS: THE MORE I HAVE BEEN ABLE to sit with, hold, and be truly present with Pain, the more ease I have experienced while moving through the healing process. Yes, facing Pain full on has actually facilitated a greater sense of lightness and a more positive connection to my true self. In facing Pain with complete presence, the negative physical sensations and the overall uncomfortable qualities of pain have been diminished. I literally feel less pain when I stand beside it and allow its presence to be fully honored. What a conundrum? During our early development, many of us have the experience of watching our family members and other close adults shy away from pain. It is no wonder that the concept of cozying up to pain is foreign to many of us. Often, the layout of our family systems in our early environment did not coach us to do what we are talking about doing here. Also, in this day and age, we are saturated by the theme of running away from pain; it is a common thread in stories from books, film, and television. So, courageous reader, this is a moment where I will ask you again to be supremely gentle with yourself whether or not you have embraced Pain in this way before.

Mindful moments

Hakomi, a mindfulness-centered somatic therapeutic modality, presents us with the concept of simply being with an uncomfortable experience where distressing affective material is present. During the process with a trained practitioner, we ask ourselves to engage our capacity to stay away from the temptation to do anything, fix anything or figure anything out. We are asked to hold the difficult experience and gently explore it with love and curiosity. An important aspect of the practitioner's job is to guide the client to remain mindful of his or her feelings and thoughts in any given moment, while not shying away from the physical discomfort experienced during the process. And although these principles are key to having a successful experience within the psychotherapeutic context, these principles are not exclusive to the modality I am referring to here.

WHEN WE ARE AS COURAGEOUS AS YOU ARE, DEAR reader, then we can cultivate the ability to sit with the discomfort by engaging in certain daily practices. After all, you have come this far on this journey by continuing to read this book, a testament to your willingness and your being curious enough about self-healing. These daily practices include many elements with regard to self-care, meditation and attending to our physical needs along the lines of exercise, good food and plenty of rest. So, let's talk a bit about one element here—meditation.

MANY HAVE THE PRECONCEIVED NOTION THAT meditation is a practice where a specific set of desired outcomes is at stake—greater balance, stillness, happiness, and so on. Let me say this: There are no stakes here and our meditation practice does not need to be focused on an outcome for its positive benefits to have a huge impact on our current well-being. One of the elements I would like to highlight here, taken directly from mindfulness-centered meditation practices, is the notion of simply paying attention to the breath. Countless clients I have worked with, myself included, report that the humble act of sitting quietly for a few minutes while listening to and being with the experience of breathing has a positive effect on their overall sense of well-being in any given moment. When we shift our attention to one simple thing, the breath, we set our intention to be with our *self* in an intimate way since the breath is life-giving and is what sustains us while we are alive. In these few moments, while paying attention to the breath, we shift the focus away from everything external to ourselves and choose to pay attention to the core of our being, while we do one thing, breathe. Our practice here is to be with the breath and allow everything else to fall away while attending to our precious spark of divinity. And although this practice is a simple one, it can be accompanied by emotions and thoughts that rise up in our stillness, taking take us away from the presence we are looking to create. This is where regular practice comes to play.

. . .

ENGAGING A PRACTICE IS AN IMPORTANT IDEA HERE since setting the intention to lie down, sit down or even go for a walk while noticing our breath might take some motivation and fortitude before we feel fully comfortable with it. My first attempts at this practice were riddled with anxiety and the rising up of automatic negative thoughts, which in turn led to negative feelings, more negative thoughts, and so on. I also found that these negative thoughts and feelings seemed to get louder when I got still and tried to settle into quiet. So, you might be asking why I would ever guide you to dip deeper into a bath of discomfort.

THE TRUTH IS, THE DISCOMFORT IS GOING TO BE there no matter what you are doing, whether or not you are paying attention to the breath or engaging in any kind of meditation practice. What is different here is that our meditation practice allows us to be with the discomfort in a safe environment for which we have set the parameters. As I have mentioned before, when we set our intention and follow through with the mission we have set before us, we are the ones in charge. As our practice becomes a regular occurrence, we notice that our capacity to find some ease in being with the distressing and uncomfortable material we are holding grows exponentially with every session.

THERE ARE MANY GREAT TEACHERS OF mindfulness-centered meditation and other types of meditation available to us located throughout our society today. If the notion of becoming a regular and skilled practitioner interests you, I suggest you find someone in your area who provides classes or even individual instruction. Also, I highly recommend searching out the work of John Kabat-Zinn, who is probably best known for mindfulness-based stress reduction (MBSR). A typical class lasts eight weeks and perhaps there is a practitioner in your area who is teaching the course in regular cycles. For our purposes here, let's explore some of the basics of paying attention to the breath since we are simply looking to be with our pain while unpacking and sorting through recent events. Our purpose in this moment is to step forward and regain our capacity to thrive, and mindfulness is a practice that can facilitate this inherent power.

THE BASICS

When I teach any type of centering meditation,

one of the first things I present to a group or a client is how we might embrace the quality of being gentle. If we are total newbies, we might think that all of the clutter I spoke of before (negative thoughts and feelings) will get in the way of our practice. The truth is that this clutter can be present without standing in our way since our practice is all about choosing where we are going to assign our attention and attending to the breath is a perfect place to start. We all have to breathe anyway so why not use the breath as a tool to lead us to a place of greater stillness and peace? When we give ourselves a break and allow everything to be just as it is without any judgment while staying away from negative self-talk, we can discover a place of respite that we can return to time and time again. Fortunately, the basics are all you need to find the ease you might be looking for during this time of suffering.

So, how do we start? In a few moments, I will ask you to put this book down after giving you some simple instructions. After you have read the instructions, take a moment, perhaps only one minute, to give it a try. First, make sure you are sitting or lying somewhere comfortably. Then, take a few breaths slowly and see what you notice. Are your breaths shallow? Are they rushed? If so, course correct and allow for a more expansive breath and perhaps slow your breathing down very gently and check in again. As I mentioned before, during my first attempts at this practice, all kinds of anxieties and thoughts came rising to the surface. Believe it or not, that is exactly what you want to happen since it will give you a signpost as to "where you are" in this moment. Continue to breathe in slowly, inhaling fully and exhaling slowly as well. Notice your breath and simply be with the breath. You may observe that intrusive thoughts and negative feelings come, and when they do, turn your attention back to the breath and simply notice the breath, plain and simple. The more you continue to do this, the more you might notice that the negative chatter seems to move farther away from you since, in this instant, you are choosing to pay attention to nothing but the breath. In essence, all of that negative "stuff" bubbling up is forced to take a backseat during this moment of self-care. You might want to have a pen and paper nearby to write down some of your impressions, especially if this is your first time engaging in this practice. Later on, even a few days from now, you can look back at these notes and see the shift that has happened if you have continued to do this a few times a day.

. . .

Now, TAKE THESE INSTRUCTIONS, GIVE THE practice a try and see what happens.

HOW WAS IT? UNCOMFORTABLE? FREEING? IN THE end, the quality or essence of the experience doesn't matter since the experience simply is what it is, nothing more. What matters here in this moment of uncertainty where you might be feeling powerless is that you have taken control by setting your intention while having performed an action in demonstration of that set intention. No external factors are driving this moment. Only you are in charge and by taking charge in this way, you have centered your entire world within the *self*, a small, humble and loving inner universe.

WITH MANY YEARS OF PRACTICE UNDER MY BELT, having studied various types of meditation, from mantra practice to Zazen sitting meditation, the connection to my breath has truly been lifesaving and turned out to be the only practice I needed when I first discovered that my spouse had been unfaithful. The grounding quality of making the world very small by my choice in any given moment, to fully attend to my spark of divinity by connecting with a mechanism that keeps me alive every day, the breath, not only created space for me to shift my perspective regarding the bitterness and anger I felt, but also afforded me the capacity to lower cortisol levels and turn my amygdala "off," so to speak.

A LITTLE NEURO-GEEK STUFF

We don't need to be a neuroscientist to understand that the notion of fight, flight, or freeze has more and more become integrated into our language with regard to our sense of humanity and how we experience and interact with the world around us. This stress response allows us to be highly attuned to perceiving danger and this ability has been honed over thousands of years.

IN TODAY'S SOCIETY, WHERE WE ARE RELENTLESSLY bombarded with negative external stimuli (just turn on the news for ten minutes and check in with how you feel), our fight, flight and freeze response is constantly being challenged. When we receive alarming news like a disclosure that our spouse has been unfaithful, for example, our limbic system goes into overdrive. All of the memories of our relationship rise to the surface with doubts, questions and fears banging on like a wretched, untalented band that just won't stop. If you know anything about the amygdala, then you know its greatest contribution is to save our lives. Yet in moments similar to what we are exploring in this book where our lives are not at stake, the amygdala does not on its own have the discernment to know the difference. Hence, the distressing affective experience occurring at the moment when we receive painful news that our loved one has cheated. For many, receiving a full and honest disclosure from an unfaithful spouse can generate these feelings, and nanoseconds after receipt of this news, the amygdala goes to work to protect us.

However, the days following this news can be very trying on our system. If we do not figuratively "turn off" the amygdala for an extended period of time, increased cortisol levels can lead to both physical and mental health problems. This overdrive of our stress response must be put in check, and to quote a very famous YouTube video, "ain't nobody got time for that!" I am oversimplifying our brain's process here, but you get the idea. Our goal, if you are still with me, is to find a way to thrive as soon as we can at the beginning of this new and perhaps unwelcome heroic journey.

. . .

So, COURAGEOUS ONE, ARE YOU READY TO LEAN into your pain? Are you ready to try this simple mindfulness practice to help you be with your entire experience? Remember to be curious, open, accepting, and loving toward yourself.

AND OF COURSE, AS ALWAYS, BE GENTLE.

7

True Self: Who Do You Think You Are?

*Our story is unique to our experience. It behooves us to tell
our story with vulnerability since this vulnerability
is always a contribution to others.*

Rather than the title of this chapter being the question we consider, the better question to ask ourselves might be, "Who are we *really*?" Who we think we are and who we truly are for many individuals are entirely different things. If we ask ourselves about the nature of our first essence upon entering this world, our first template so to speak, what unknowns about this nature come to the surface of our awareness? Who were we before the world got to us? Who were we before our family system had an influence on us, before countless disappointments, acute stressors and negative experiences impacted our first template? I could go on and on about the things that shape and inform who we become from a developmental point of view, but let's keep it simple. Have you ever truly asked yourself the question, "Who am I?" In the past, I had asked this question in a benign way with very little willingness to go deep for the answer. I had never asked it fully until I began studying to become a therapist. For our purposes here, let's really hold the question and simply allow for any answer to come to us. If you are willing to join me on this quest, this is no doubt a courageous move, dear reader. Yet if you are willing to take this mission, I can assure you that answers will arrive at the doorstep of your being without fail.

WITH ALL OF THIS IN MIND, WOULDN'T IT BE exciting to take a peek back at our first template to get to examine the purest elements of our makeup? Well, courageous reader, we can, especially now that you have been reading this book with a modicum of self-study under your belt.

. . .

WHEN WE BEGIN TO EXPLORE AND PERHAPS EVEN begin to understand who we really are, we set ourselves on a path that some might call a path to enlightenment. I am inclined to call it something along the lines of a path to self-discovery since, for my brain, that path seems a little more doable. However, it can be said that enlightenment is a by-product of any kind of self-study and quest for personal development. So, if we are going to continue to discover new things about ourselves, it means we need to study ourselves; study ourselves with the gentle curiosity we would have if we were unpacking a strange, magical and unfamiliar object. In the end, we truly cannot fail to become more enlightened: more enlightened about how we interact with the world around us, more enlightened with regard to how we engage our relationships with others and most importantly, more enlightened about how we see and experience our truest sense of self.

A CAMBRIDGE DICTIONARY DEFINITION FOR enlightenment is "the state of understanding something," which begs the question for me, do I fully need to understand something in order for it to have a positive and lasting impact on my life path? In Buddhism, enlightenment is considered to be a spiritual state where everything is understood and our suffering ends. I was chuckling as I wrote these words as I was certainly not shooting for that endgame when I presented this work to the world. However, can we find our innate resilience in times of loss and uncertainty so that our experience is more buoyant and filled with ease? Can we allow space for courageous openheartedness that in the end invites the presence of Grace? I don't think so. I know so. I know so from personal experience and I know so from the countless individuals who have reported their own version of this experience to me over the years.

Bullshit

So, how does this self-study begin? If you haven't ever sat with a therapist or a coach in order to get to the bottom of things that are troubling you, then you might not have had the experience of having an objective listener use his or her critical thinking skills to challenge you on our bullshit. Yes, I said your bullshit. I've got bullshit that at times keeps me from finding clarity—as do you. We all carry around sacks of it in varying weights and sizes. Until we are courageous enough to unpack it either with the help of a professional or by truly challenging ourselves to fully observe and explore it with the curiosity I spoke of earlier, our bullshit will continue to be a barrier to our ability to thrive.

HERE IS THE THING ABOUT THRIVING: MANY PEOPLE think they are thriving yet find themselves stressed out on a daily basis. They repeatedly complain about other people and their actions, schlep around bitterness and speak incessantly about the shit state of the world. They try and convince themselves and others that they are on top of their game and often argue about this untruth to the bitter end. This is not thriving. Period. This is sleepwalking and until we are awake enough to see this, we suffer—even if we are not aware of our own suffering because it has become an ingrained way of being for us. Perhaps an in-depth discussion of this particular subject is best left for another book altogether since, again, we could go on and on about this topic.

THE SIMPLE TRUTH IS, IF WE DON'T HAVE A GOOD meter for sussing out our own bullshit, then we may need the help and support of someone else, and if you are starting out on this program of self-study, I suggest you go and get that support, just until you get your bullshit meter tuned up.

· · ·

STEP UP AND HAVE A LOOK

So, here we are being asked to take a hard look at our own bullshit. Brené Brown is the inspiration here. If you read her work or listen to her speak, you know she has rolled up her sleeves and wrestled with her own bullshit in a way that is most courageous. So courageous that she talks about it on the world stage—fierceness at its best.

HOWEVER, WHETHER OR NOT YOU ARE INTO Brené Brown's work is neither here nor there. The essence of what I'm speaking to is that if you wish to bring your greatest self to any arena, it is imperative that you do some kind of self-study. As Socrates said, "Know thyself." It's a pretty benign phrase, overused and somewhat hackneyed, yet it holds the essence of what this book is about: getting to know yourself while under the duress of your current experience, which in turn might help you reclaim your power and sense of purpose.

THE THING WE HAVE TO TUSSLE WITH HERE IS THAT this *knowing* begins with the empty space of *not knowing*. I was sitting in a big puddle of not knowing when starting to write this book. The big question that arose for me was, how does one navigate a perceived horrible experience while remaining buoyant and present without some understanding of the self? Can it be done? Is it possible to be crushed by the figurative steamroller of loss, stand up and regain the forward momentum needed to build a future where one is not afraid to embrace joy, abundance and love? Is it at all possible to do this if we do not possess a profuse understanding of the self? And if we decide it is possible to take on this task without the understanding we are concerned with here, how do we actually get our shit together and get a move on? The how, I believe, begins with the type of self-study we are exploring in this book.

THE CYNIC

Upon reflection of everything that we have observed together thus far, courageous reader, I must disclose that I remain a gentle cynic. However, harsh cynicism most definitely used to be part of my makeup. Some of you might be having the experience of reading what I have written so far and are feeling your harsh cynic rise to the surface. I will say this—it was not until I began to release my cynical way of thinking and take a risk by being softer and gentler toward my *self* that I was able to breathe in the experience of healing with some ease. Yes, it was a risk to be gentle toward myself in the beginning, as my tendency had always been to be driven and rigid. Hitting the eject button on resentment and anger and allowing space for the greatest amount of self-love one can muster is truly the path to thriving and happiness, no doubt. In order to write this book, I had to do this very quickly. One of the most remarkable and surprising aspects of this bounce back and leap into my resiliency was that it happened in an organic and somewhat unplanned way. I love surprises, but this experience surprised me more than anything ever has in my entire life.

HOURS AFTER MY SPOUSE'S DISCLOSURE, I FOUND myself waking from the fog of "what (the fuck) just happened?" Remarkably, my *self* got in first gear and made it clear that I needed to get in alignment with who I really am. I knew that the best outcome for me meant that I needed to return to my meditation practice, exercise, eat well and NOT begin indulging in any self-destructive behaviors. If I fell into old habits, my now ramped-up journey of self-discovery might have figuratively ended up looking like an empty raft floating chaotically down a raging river; I'm supposed to be in the raft, navigating the rapids, but somewhere near the beginning of that perilous journey, I bailed. And as I have disclosed before, I have been there and done that—no need for a repeat performance.

THE TRUTH ABOUT NAVIGATING DIFFICULT TIMES IS that anyone can connect to a sense of ease, even when we are observing the type of difficult time we are exploring in this book. My sense of ease came from (1), practices that have helped me maintain balance, and (2), continuing to engage gentle curiosity when looking at myself. A large dose of tuning into the pain with a lighter heart when unpacking the hard stuff meant that I was able to steer away from rumination on how "bad" things were. Everything I have learned and explored about myself in recent years had prepared me for this moment and you, courageous reader, have access to everything I am speaking to here. So, let's explore this thing called self-study.

TAKING INVENTORY

Self-study is not unlike opening a large tome that is solely about you and setting the intention to read every last word. That might sound like a daunting task and maybe even an unpleasant one. However, self-study infused with the kind of curiosity I have spoken of before means that we are engaging the process with a light and playful heart. When we find a calm place from where we are able to observe our "stuff" with openness and acceptance, we can then do some unpacking and gentle sorting.

AS A MENTAL HEALTH PROFESSIONAL, MY BRAIN CAN sometimes be geared toward deconstructing a problem and looking for solutions. It is the way I was trained and it is certainly a useful tool within the confines of my profession, but let's put on the brakes here. We are asking ourselves to engage in some self-study, not deconstruct a problem someone else is holding—we are here to study our *self*. Whenever I work with a client, I am often introducing the notion of self-study. From the start of our work together, we seek to infuse this self-study with gentleness, a sprinkle of lightheartedness and a willingness to allow anything (thoughts, feelings, etc.) to rise up. We embrace this study in a mindful and loving way and each client is guided to bring the essence of what we do together to his or her alone time. And so begins the initial taking of inventory.

Mental health

In taking inventory and unpacking the pieces of the fabulous jigsaw puzzle that is who we really are, we also need to consider our mental health during the course of this process. Although my opinions on the topic may not resonate with everyone, I urge you to consider that your mental health is an infinitely important element that will directly impact your ability to study yourself fully and achieve the outcome you seek while reading this book. I feel quite certain in saying that most people on this planet have experienced bouts of depression and/or have fought with and tried to push away anxiety on some level. We have all felt the deep pain associated with grief and loss. As human beings, we experience phobias and fears, challenges that create barriers to our ability to thrive and through it all, most of us manage to make it through.

If you have never been to a therapist and you are reading this book while experiencing a mixed bag of all of the things I mentioned above, get a therapist. I repeat, get a therapist. I don't say this lightly while writing this. We all need support in times of extreme difficulty and going it alone can mean that the trajectory of our success might be greatly diminished. If in doubt, read the chapter

"Shouting Out for Support," where I discuss how the essence of our healing is born out of our sense of connection—connection to loving, helping professionals included.

WHEN IT COMES TO DEFINING OR SETTING OUT TO make some determination about who we think we really are, one thing that I am very opinionated about and I'm going to stress here emphatically is that if we have been given any mental health diagnosis such as a generalized anxiety disorder or major depression, it behooves us to *not* identify with that diagnosis. Let me explain what I mean. I absolutely do not mean that we should ignore the diagnosis or forget about it. What I mean is we should observe the diagnosis as an observation we have been provided by a medical professional about our current experience with regard to our mental health. We must observe the diagnosis as one piece of our complex and beautiful jigsaw puzzle that simply needs putting in place so that we have a greater understanding of how we currently experience the world.

THE DIAGNOSIS IS BY NO MEANS WHO WE ARE AT OUR truest essence, nor is it a burden we should amplify and carry as if it were excess baggage we wish we didn't have. Sure, we might truly wish that we were not anxious or depressed, and if this is your current experience directly related to your current circumstances, consider that your wholeness and completeness would not be whole and complete without this current experience. Did you get that? This experience is fully resonant with your wholeness and completeness—period. I remember when my therapist said that to me, my mind was blown!

I WAS GIVEN A GENERALIZED ANXIETY DISORDER diagnosis (GAD) during a particularly dark time in my life and before this diagnosis, instead of turning to skills that might have ensured my remaining buoyant through this challenging time, I turned to alcohol. One of the greatest blessings I received upon being presented with this diagnosis was the presence of a therapist who said that observing the diagnosis can be somewhat like taking a personality test and finding out you are an introvert. It is part of who you are, but it does not define you. From there, she helped me to view my wholeness and completeness like one might view a large and beautiful painting: there are lots of colors and shapes, some colors we don't like, some shapes we think are ugly, but when we step back and look at the entire work of art representing who we really are, it is dynamic and fiercely beautiful.

You might remember RAIN from the chapter "Out of the Darkness." Non-identification is a practice that can truly ground us in who we really are while giving us the capacity to observe all of the external stuff flying around us. We might, if we are not careful, begin to identify with this stuff. For example, as soon as we say, "I *am* bipolar" or "I *am* anxious," we are fully identifying with those phrases, and in my opinion, giving vibration to those phrases is as detrimental and harmful as saying out loud the words, "I *am* ugly" or "I *am* worthless."

So, what's the trick to non-identification while still being able to observe the challenges we hold? From the start, we can ask questions like, "How will I hold feeling anxious today while I continue to contribute in a unique way to the world around me?" When we phrase the question in this way, it already contains an element of non-identification since we are declaring our intention to *hold* the anxiety rather than *be* the anxiety. Do you see the difference?

. . .

The good I AM

If we are looking for strength-focused ways to identify with qualities we possess, "I am" statements are more powerful than we can ever imagine. As soon as we make the declaration of being, "I am," we are giving vibration to not only the quality of our current state, but we are also solidifying that state of being with a cognitive process. Our brains are wired to believe what we tell it and if we begin solidifying anything about ourselves by the use of "I am" statements, doesn't it behoove us to make sure these declarations support our well-being rather than detract from it? If you have decided to stay with me on the idea that we are all whole and complete and truly have our own answers, doesn't it stand to reason that any negative input generated by ourselves and our negativity in any given moment is not actually the truth? You might argue the inverse of this is true since we are going for the same result with intentionally setting forth positive input with our "I am" statements. I will remind you again that we are looking to reclaim our power, not undermine it. So, don't play devil's advocate, and put away that cynic we spoke of earlier.

. . .

IN THIS CHAPTER, WE ARE EXAMINING WHO WE really are. As you continue to study your *self*, perhaps you are finding that the core of who you really are is made of something luminous and intrinsically good—love. If we are going to get our brains working for us rather than against us, let's initiate cognitive processes that start or continue to encourage forward momentum. Love is like the battery pack for that cognitive process, so let's be loving toward ourselves.

ON THE FLIP SIDE, IF WE FIND OURSELVES IN THE throes of negative thought patterns that are pulling us down as we uncover and explore the experience we are investigating in this book, it is up to us to discover a means to shift away from these negative thoughts. Otherwise, we are at risk of remaining with the status quo, steeping in our misery and suffering. By now, courageous reader, I assume that you are reading this book so that increased levels of misery and suffering in the face of loss and uncertainty do not become your only story. I will mention again the notion of mental health—if you think you need a therapist during this time, then you probably do, so go get one! If you're feeling that connecting with a life coach will help you gain the momentum you seek, go and get a life coach. It's quite a simple process and you can begin taking the first steps toward finding support before the end of today.

A PROCESS

So, brave one, who are you really? One way of identifying some qualities you possess that are in direct alignment with who you really are comes from a body of work by a powerful and gifted woman by the name of Maria Nemeth. She is a world-class coach, author of *The Energy of Money* and *Mastering Life's Energies* and was introduced to me by my former spouse—something for which I still have gratitude since I consider her gifts to be a huge contribution to the world. Ms. Nemeth developed a tool for identifying one's own standards of integrity and I have used a modified version of this with coaching and therapy clients for years. First and foremost, I have applied this tool to my own life and have found it to be enlightening, to say the least. Exploring our standards of integrity can give us some insight into qualities or traits that we might want to foster and share with the world. Her premise is that if we admire these traits in others, then it stands to reason that we must possess them ourselves. Otherwise, we would not be able to recognize them and it is this connection to and resonance with our integrity that is an echo of our wholeness and completeness.

IN ITS SIMPLEST FORM, THIS EXERCISE IN EXPLORING our standards of integrity goes something like this:

1. GRAB A COUPLE OF SHEETS OF PLAIN OR LINED paper. Take one piece and write down the names of seven to ten people you admire. The people on this list can be family members, friends, colleagues, famous people, a character from a story in a book or film, anyone really. They can be alive or deceased and you don't necessarily have to know them personally.

2. AFTER COMPLETING YOUR LIST, WRITE DOWN qualities that you admire in these individuals next to their names. Some individuals may have one quality you admire, while others may have multiple. One individual from my standards of integrity list is my grandmother Shirley. Since I never called her Shirley, I would write Grams on my list simply because of my personal connection to her. An abbreviated version of my list looks something like this:

```
            people I admire

Grams - talented, funny, kind,
loving, energetic

K. Reeves - selfless, grounded

B. Brown - courageous, brilliant,
strong, bold

Mom - talented, creative, loving,
giving, luminous

Bran - wise
```

Notice that the qualities I placed next to the names are one-word summations of something I admire about the person. If you find it difficult to express a specific quality in just one word, write a short phrase describing what you are going for and spend some time discovering what that word might be and add it later.

3. NOW THAT YOU HAVE YOUR LIST COMPILED, LOOK over the words you have written here. Do you need to add or refine some? You can have as many words on your list as you like. Once you feel your list is complete, it's time to use some discernment since we are going to choose five qualities that resonate with us most strongly in this present moment. Circle the five most resonant words/qualities and when

you feel certain about your choices, pull out your other piece of paper. Note: don't worry about or stress over narrowing your choices to only five—you will understand why in a minute.

people I admire

Grams - talented, funny, kind, loving, (energetic)

K. Reeves - selfless, (grounded)

B. Brown - courageous, brilliant, strong, (bold)

Mom - talented, (creative, loving,) giving, luminous

Bran - wise

4. On your second sheet of paper, draw a fairly large circle in the center. Think of the circle as being a container for holding something sacred. When you are ready, write your selected five words inside of that circle. You can simply write them as a list straight down the center, write them around the edge of the circle, fill the entire circle with the words; it doesn't matter. Be creative.

5. IN THE FINAL PART OF THIS EXERCISE, WE ARE simply going to write a couple of phrases: one at

the top of your sheet of paper and one at the bottom. At the top of the page, the first phrases are: *These are my standards of integrity. I am.* At the bottom of the page, you will write: *I know this to be true because I can see them in others.* The final product should look something like this:

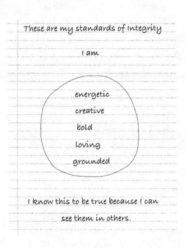

These are my standards of integrity

I am

energetic
creative
bold
loving
grounded

I know this to be true because I can see them in others.

Have a look at what you have written here. Can you recognize these qualities as being fully yours? Are you able to read what is before you and believe it? Even if you have questions about some of them belonging to you, attend to the ones or even one that fully resonates.

THIS IS A TOOL THAT YOU MIGHT BRING TO YOUR therapy or coaching session. Perhaps you might discuss this with a friend over lunch. Our purpose here is to highlight qualities we possess that play roles in elevating our strength and resilience. You can return to this exercise again and again and remind yourself of these qualities when you are feeling out of alignment with who you really are.

ALSO, IT IS IMPORTANT TO NOTE THAT YOU POSSESS all of the qualities you have selected so you might find that your list shifts over time; some qualities remain on the list much of the time while others shift and change depending on what you are observing in the present moment. Have fun observing these strengths and putting them into play in your daily life.

SO, MY DEAR READER, HERE WE ARE AT THE END OF this chapter. Take some time with your fabulous self to let this information soak in and become integrated into your experience. I am always reminding myself to remember the wisdom of great teachers when I am examining any element of self-study, so here's one for you: John Kabat-Zinn says, "All the suffering, stress and addiction comes from not realizing that you are already what you are looking for." Remind yourself again that you have everything you need and possess your own answers as you move forward from here. Remember that idea regarding our wholeness and completeness we were looking at earlier? This would be a moment to remind ourselves of that fact.

AND AS CONTINUE THROUGH THIS BOOK, ENGAGING in heroic self-study, I will remind you again to continue to be gentle with yourself.

8

Rebuilding

We may not achieve the life we have created in our mind's eye but if we are willing and open, we might have a life that far exceeds the one we were planning.

B y now, you might have already begun to experience some healing as you have moved through this book. And as you begin to notice that you are finding greater balance and greater attunement to the self, the notion of rebuilding a life, whether it be alone, with your partner or perhaps even with a new partner, is probably taking a front seat with you. On this drive through life, if we take time to pull into rest stops along the way, we give ourselves time and space for the healing process to fully come to fruition. And not unlike a long drive toward a destination, sometimes we really do need to figuratively pull over and take a break.

HEALING IS NOT A PROCESS TO BE HURRIED. HAVE you ever scraped your knee or cut your finger and been able to rush that healing along? The healing process simply takes as long as it takes. Even when we are children and are highly prone to accidents like scraped knees and elbows, the healing of those wounds does not happen overnight. So why do we think it should be any different with emotional, psychological and spiritual healing? This again brings me to the idea of being gentle, which I have pointed to multiple times in this book. Healing requires a gentle and loving hand. Whether the healing process is being guided by a professional or if we are embarking on this path while flying completely solo, healing must be allowed to occur at its own pace and on its own terms, not at all unlike those scraped knees and elbows.

HOWEVER, OUR MINDFUL ENGAGEMENT IN THE healing process is what keeps the tank full and the vehicle of our self moving forward with ever gaining momentum. Have you ever noticed that about a healing process? As we reconnect with our sense of balance and find ourselves in an emotional, psychological and spiritual place where we begin to actually feel good again, it seems that the momentum toward an overall positive sense of well-being increases. We feel better and better with gaining momentum. If we stay with that momentum and do not create barriers to its inherent flow, we arrive at our destination with sometimes a surprising clarity and an unexpected sense of ease. I have had this experience and while sitting smack in the middle of it, I have felt puzzled for a moment (or thirty) until I reflect upon and acknowledge my contribution to reinstating my sense of wholeness and completeness. Even with years of self-study under my belt, remembering that my true self is always whole and complete can still confound me. Reminder: Let's acknowledge ourselves and remember that in these instants of self-reflection, we are allowing ourselves to be fully present to our current experience and not checking out. This is no small feat and after all, our true self knew we would get there anyway, however long it took.

So, what does it take for us now that we have begun to feel the forward momentum of healing and actually begin to rebuild? Some of you reading this book right now might feel like you need to start over completely. In our minds, starting over often means that we tell ourselves we need to rebuild our confidence, rebuild our self-esteem, rebuild a life where we must now fend for ourselves alone and without support. We exacerbate the discomfort of this experience by believing this is doubly true since we are no longer partnered. Is this true or is it simply the story we tell ourselves? We are often told this story since we see it in literature, movies, TV shows, and so on. This story has been dramatized in more ways than we can count. With that in mind, here comes a challenge.

To set the stage, I am going to self-disclose and then make a bold statement regarding this notion of rebuilding that may not resonate with you at first. With that being said, I challenge you to stay with me for a little while longer.

When I first separated from my spouse, I held the story that something had been "done to me." I was a victim and because of my spouse's actions, I held the story that my life was like a box containing one thousand Lego pieces, each representing all aspects of my entire experience. In my story, this box had been thrown over the edge of a cliff. In order to thrive and rebuild this sad state of a life, I would need to hit the reset button and start completely over. For a minute or two (actually, I held this belief for a couple of weeks), I believed that I had no foundation from which to begin this process of rebuilding. The business we had created together would now be defunct. The life of happiness and abundance I had planned for was never going to happen ... oh, the stories I told myself during that time. And do you know what the main by-product of telling myself these stories was? Suffering. Plain and simple. And if I was the one telling those stories, who was creating the suffering? Me. Not my spouse, me.

So here is where the challenge comes in when looking at the idea of rebuilding. Read the next, italicized passage carefully and with all of the curiosity, openness, acceptance and love you can muster, take it in and see what you notice on the inside of yourself. Chucking your judgment in the garbage right now will be helpful as well—you can always go and collect it again later if you have decided that you still need it.

The stories I was telling myself, the beliefs that I had regarding my need to completely rebuild from a nonexistent foundation were all derived from my own bullshit.

BREATHE AND TAKE THAT IN FOR SECOND.

BREATHE AGAIN.

YOU MAY FIND THAT YOUR MIND WANTS TO COME UP with a laundry list of reasons why rebuilding from nothing is the only way to frame how the next part of your journey will appear. You might even justify using that word when reading about my story. However, when I was able to sit back, take a breath and actually observe what was occurring in physical reality, I realized that I did not need to rebuild anything at all. Since the foundation of my life was already there, there was no rebuilding from a nonexistent foundation. If I was to collude with the belief that I was starting over with nothing, would I not be diminishing my own spark of divinity in some way? If I was to align with these negative beliefs, doesn't it stand to reason that I would be negating the inherent, Universe-given qualities that I have argued we all possess? In order to step back into thrive mode, we really must hold this question with an open heart and open mind.

If we draw negative conclusions about our worthiness and the fullness of our being in direct response to an adverse experience, in order to stave off the downward spiral into colluding with the negative beliefs, my feeling is that we must begin by fully acknowledging our inherent worth right from the start. In doing so, we tether our mind to the truth, the truth that our inherent value is a constant that cannot be shifted. And as we do this specific and arduous work, we must ask ourselves powerful questions that continuously affirm our worth.

Am I fully worthy just by the very nature of my being here? Yes. When my spouse cheated on me, was I robbed of my intelligence, resourcefulness and creativity? No. Do I still have connections with people who love and care about me? Yes. There are endless questions we can ask ourselves that point to and remind us of our inherent value. Search for yours and ask them in a direct, uninhibited way.

Are you getting what I'm saying here?

. . .

THIS TINY EXERCISE IS POWERFUL, YET WE MUST challenge ourselves to keep the cynic out of the conversation. I set the stage in this way so that perhaps in a moment of stillness and maybe even during the course of only one breath, you might begin to shift the way you think regarding the way you frame your current experience. Remember, you are the only one who can make that shift for yourself—no one else can do this for you.

WHEN WE GET DOWN TO IT, IT REALLY IS AS SIMPLE as this: we can play the victim or we can choose to be the hero of our own story—the choice is exclusively ours.

AND AS WE COME TO THE CLOSE OF THIS CHAPTER, what occurs to you? Is the cynic present? Have you managed to keep your higher self actively engaged while moving through this experience? Did you give yourself enough time to actually breathe in the suggestions I made earlier? If you are finding this process difficult, remember my suggestions from earlier chapters. Find a therapist who can be your accountability buddy. Find a certified and experienced coach who is unafraid of calling you on your bullshit. Once you have put the polish on your ability to discern what self-talk is serving your highest purpose, you will find that you can hold this experience in a new and more powerful way. The work here is rigorous and I don't imagine since you have read this far in the book, you are expecting some type of easy button.

So, here's to you, courageous one. Keep it up. You're doing great!

9

Shouting Out for Support

When we bring our presence to all beings, we bring a whole world of experience that embodies a unique contribution to all who cross our path.

L et's remind ourselves that many of us are willing to be fully present to those in need, whether they be family members, close friends or even strangers in distress. The beautiful thing about this fact is that it is in our true nature to seek protection and protect those around us during difficult times—it's simply the way we are designed. If we are willing to be present to others experiencing a moment of need, then we must connect to our own humility and learn to reach out for support when we, too, are suffering.

. . .

As an introvert, my alone time is precious to me. When I set my intention to be alone, it is often for the purpose of figuratively recharging my batteries. Spending time reading, writing, meditating, eating chocolate chip cookies with a side of Netflix, all of it being engaged with a certain amount of quietude, helps me to feel balanced and ready to interact with others. Most importantly, this type of self-care affords me the capacity to be a contribution to the world around me.

Upon separation from my spouse, I claimed almost three months of complete alone time, moving to Vancouver, Canada, to begin writing this book. During this time, I purposefully interacted with very few people and spent a lot of time exploring the city quietly, staying indoors on rainy days to write and reflect while pretty much keeping to myself. It was blissful. Creating this space gave me ample time to process what had happened, check in with myself in the here and now and begin contemplating what the future might hold for me. I fully understand that claiming three months of alone time is not for everybody and although this chapter is about exploring the idea of welcoming support, I am reminded that support from our inner being is also something to be sought after, hence my need for a long break that included plenty of alone time.

AT THE START OF THIS NEW LIFE CHAPTER, THAT DAY as I drove away from my spouse after receiving heartbreaking news, I wondered if I was going to remain resilient through this experience or if I would crash and burn. My sense of self had been challenged and I imagine like any other human being might do, I questioned whether or not some of my identity and ideas about who I am were completely untrue. I was a married man—this is something I considered to be a fact about myself. Being married was part of my identity and as you might already know, identity is often married to the ego. So, I was perched at the edge of a potential trap and thankfully, I didn't step in. As I navigated the weedy undergrowth of negative thoughts cropping up in my brain, I knew that I didn't want to lose my sense of self. In a most basic yet principled way, I understood that the self not only resides at the very core of my being, but it is also the core, and with some modicum of clarity, I started to gain some deeper connection to this core and release the barrage of thoughts that I would come to label as monkey mind.

It is my belief that we get in contact with who we really are in moments of silence and during the acquisition of quiet time. Since I wanted to call upon support from my inner being near the beginning of this journey, quiet and silence were absolutely necessary so that I could be in close contact with my *self*. In spite of the noise and chatter going on in my head and the hurling of doubts and fears with each passing minute, I chose to claim a sacred space of quietude and embrace the silence accompanying that quietude. This was a nonnegotiable stance that I am grateful I held strongly from the start. We will explore the idea of silence and its attributes in the next chapter, so read on if the practice of being in silence and what it might afford you is of interest.

Support from our inner being and support from loving friends and family members need to be in balance for us to have the experience of thriving through any difficult time. We find this place of balance when we ask for support from both our inner being and from those who love us. Many of us require solitude to connect to our inner being, but isolation in excess can mean that we make ourselves not available or open to loving input and acknowledgments from the people who care about us. Our brain needs connection with others in order to thrive and it behooves us to stay connected to those who love us while we are suffering, whether that be our biological family or the family we have consciously aligned with on our life path. On the flip side, if we rely solely on input from others to guide us, we lose our autonomy and ability to self-determine, thus relinquishing our power, which can lead to even greater uncertainty. Balance, although not always an easy one to strike, plays a leading role in our capacity to continue our forward momentum while remaining in touch with our best self. There is no perfect equation for attaining the type of balance I am speaking to here and in this moment of uncertainty, it is helpful to remind ourselves that there are truly no wrong turns, no wrong answers, only experiences.

Since there is no such thing as perfect balance in this situation, what kind of balance might we be seeking? I imagine there will be as many different answers to this question as there are different people on the planet who have faced this predicament. If we are mindful that every element from our environment has an impact on us both internally and externally, then we have a point of discernment from which we can make good choices for ourselves. If we envision alone time and engagement with others as polarities, we can observe that they are interdependent of one another and too much of one means that the other is out of balance. In other chapters, we explore the notion of taking care of ourselves with practices and rituals that keep us healthy spiritually, psychologically and emotionally with many of these activities to be done on our own, but let's look more closely at asking for support from others.

WHAT DO WE NEED TO KNOW ABOUT THIS NOTION of connecting to others during our time of need? One thing I know for certain is that when our ego steers us from calling upon support or even accepting the offered support from others, our humility in these moments is lacking. When we do not accept the support offered us and when we fail to call upon the support of others in difficult times, it is almost like we are saying, "I got this and I don't need anybody." If we set our intention with this vibration, inevitably, we will find ourselves alone and that kind of isolation not only amplifies the sense of loss we are experiencing, it takes us directly away from our birthright, which is to thrive.

. . .

A DEAR FRIEND, WORLD-CLASS COACH AND AUTHOR, Kemi Nekvapil, has written a marvelous book centered on the principle of asking called *The Gift of Asking*, where she lovingly explores the notion of vulnerability and the humility required to ask for support. Although the book is targeted around the empowerment of women, I highly recommend this read to anyone, including men and perhaps even especially men, since classically, men are not often socialized to ask for help and support with any sense of ease.

SHE BEGS US TO EXPLORE WITH OPEN AND GENTLE curiosity what we are not asking for and why we are not asking for it. Many of us feel that if we are asking for support from someone, we are placing a burden on the person from whom we are asking for this support. Our minds can fill with negative thoughts surrounding the notion of equating asking with weakness and neediness. When we collude with these thoughts, we find ourselves believing that we will not receive what we are asking for and this, in turn, can lead to feelings of shame and humiliation. The longer we stay in this headspace, the more our sense of worthiness is chipped away and the more our sense of worthiness is diminished, the more at risk we are for this pattern to become cyclic and a self-fulfilling prophecy. We will inevitably find ourselves alone—not at all what we are looking for here, is it? With our needs being unmet and carrying a weakened sense of self, we can begin to feel the pangs of resentment and the uprising of anger that only can leave us feeling disconnected from the light we fundamentally possess. But as Ms. Nekvapil so beautifully points out, if we allow our anger to invade our presence and gnaw away inside of us, it can alter us in a way that is detrimental to our well-being. Stagnant anger that is not shifted into some form of productive energy ravages our spirit and limits our ability to see our life with clarity.

LOOKING FURTHER AT THE BENEFIT THAT COMES with asking for support, Ms. Nekvapil reminds us that when we ask for support and when our needs are met, we are able to live our lives in such a way that the fullness of our being is ever-present. How marvelous is this concept? When our needs are met, the quality of our being is expanded. We can *be* more and with every breath, we can find the ease and grace that is our entitlement. In this moment of darkness, dear reader, when we have discovered that our chosen partner has failed to be faithful to us, is this not the prime moment for us to be attuned to the fullest expression of ourselves so that we may remain buoyant and connected to our sense of power? It is in this moment that our greatest opportunity for rejuvenation is fully present since the seedbed from which we will cultivate the rest of our lives is ready for fresh planting.

ASKING REQUIRES US TO TAP INTO NOT ONLY OUR humility and vulnerability but our courage as well. Our courage and our access to courage is our birthright and as I have stated before, it is not something we must search for outside of ourselves. So, remember the practical approach to finding your courage I spoke of in the first chapter and allow your courage to carry you toward asking for support.

VALUE

A seminal question that all of us need to ask ourselves that is posed by Ms. Nekvapil in her book is, "Do I value myself enough to ask?" She states that "action changes everything" and in this time of suffering where we are feeling the great expanse of loss and the jagged edges of uncertainty, is this not a prime time to connect to our humility? It is highly probable that we are deeply unsatisfied with the current landscape of our life and if we are going to provide fodder for our seedbed to grow and eventually flourish, is this not a crucial moment to act? It is true that our fears can cause us to freeze. Our worries that we will receive a "no" can dredge up our worst sense of shame and hopelessness. Hopefully though by now, we understand that not asking for nor accepting the support offered to us will leave us trudging this rugged path alone. My feeling is that this moment is begging for us to find connection especially since we have been thrust into an unwelcome void that can by its very nature feel lonely, empty and lacking in the light we might so desperately need. That light can be brought by the support of others—think about it.

SOMETHING TO REMEMBER HERE IS THAT WHATEVER the length of our relationship, five weeks, five months or five years plus, our brains have been attuned to the presence of another and now that person is not part of our daily experience if we have separated from them. And even if we have not separated from them, there is now more than likely a figurative yet palpable distance between us and our partner. So, courageous reader, if you and I agree, then we fully understand that asking for support is imperative in this moment.

WHEN I WAS MAKING THE TRANSITION FROM LIVING in Vancouver to returning to Italy, there was a period of about ten days where I would be visiting my hometown. Since my spouse and I had rented out our townhouse, I needed places to stay in order to not spend a lot of money staying in hotels or Airbnb flats. It was not at all easy for me to contact a couple of my friends and ask for the support of staying with them for a few days. The first thing that came up for me was that I was going to be a burden in their already busy lives. This story was of course not true and hanging with that story would only have created a barrier to receiving support from friends who love and value my presence in their lives.

ONE OF THE MOST IMPACTFUL IDEAS I RECEIVED from reading *The Gift of Asking* is the awareness that when we ask for support from someone, we are honoring the wholeness and completeness of that person. We are, in essence, acknowledging their capacity to be a contribution to the world. In my view, when we elevate someone in this way, we are in turn elevating ourselves.

If we can find a way to shift our mindset and *heartset* away from a sense of lack and turn toward the willingness to receive the abundance inherently ours, we tap into our best self. When we shout out for support, we are also calling forth that person's capacity for tuning into their best self. My belief is that this shift is one of the most empowering and loving actions we can take. Remind yourself of a time where someone you love and care about asked for support. I imagine for most of us, it has been relatively easy to step up and be acutely present. It is how we are designed and our interconnectedness is like the battery pack that fuels our ability to be present and loving.

Now, take a breath.

Here we are at the end of this chapter having explored the idea of being vulnerable, acknowledging our worthiness and shaking off any barriers that keep us from asking for and receiving the support we fundamentally deserve. It is my sincere wish that these words have got you pondering and perhaps reconsidering some long-held beliefs that are keeping you from receiving support and, more importantly, keeping from asking for support.

So, COURAGEOUS READER, ARE YOU READY TO ASK for support? I hope so!

10

Silence and Creating Space

*Can you be comfortable in your own company
without distraction or external stimulus?
We want to know who you are in these moments
and we want you to bring that way of being to our presence.*

So many of us spend an entire lifetime surrounded by copious amounts of hustle and bustle while carrying around emotional and psychological clutter of which we often have no full awareness. In alignment with what society tells us to do, we mind-numbingly participate in the drudgery of nine-to-five jobs, raise kids, fill our calendars with dates, appointments, meetings, and we do this in a sleep-like state. We become entangled in preparing meals for our partner and loved ones, planning vacations, playing on the Internet, running errands, doing chores year in and year out. I think you get the point I am trying to make by now: Many of us are sleepwalking our way through this lifetime following a long-established template for a way to live that is completely out of alignment with actual thriving. Whether we are raising a family or are now finding ourselves thrust into the uncomfortable void of being single again with no significant other, let's explore the notion of how decluttering our lives might create enough space so that we discover the foundation of real healing. This healing begins with what some of you might find to be unexpected.

SILENCE

It is uncomfortable for many people to be with themselves in complete silence. Are you comfortable with being alone with yourself uninterrupted for any lengthy period of time? The first time I practiced silence, I set my intention to find comfort in being totally alone with my *self* for three consecutive days. I had this idea that I needed to practice silence in one giant heap in order to activate the type of spiritual supernova I was seeking at the time. Even though I did not have the experience that I had imagined the first time around, I am grateful that I figuratively went through the motions. Now my practice of silence transpires in much smaller measures, even occurring on a daily basis.

THIS FIRST QUEST IN THE PRACTICE OF SILENCE happened on an expedition to the Great Smoky Mountains National Park in my beautiful home state of Tennessee. Weeks before, I had decided that I needed to have attempted this mystical practice and it needed to occur in the perfect place that was perfectly remote so that this meditative experience could occur in the perfect setting for achieving the perfect level of zen. I know, you can already see the crash and burn coming, but stay with me. Upon arrival, it was pouring with rain and in a quirky but beautiful cabin I had rented in a remote area of the mountains, I settled in and thought, "This is perfect! I will have no reason to go outside anyway, so this silence thing should be a breeze!" And so, I remained in silence for three days. It was glorious … at least on the first day. On that first day, I allowed my mind to wander, listened to the rain and stayed away from the Internet and television. There was a large hot tub on the deck overlooking the lush mountain forest where I soaked, drank Mayfield milk and ate almost an entire package of break and bake cookies. I was completely blissed out, as they say. Silence was a cozy buddy holding me tight while keeping me feeling safe and sound. Perfect.

ON THE SECOND DAY, I WOKE UP FEELING RESTLESS and uncomfortable. I had the urge to get on the Internet or turn on the TV for some kind of background noise and distraction but ended up making the decision to continue with my practice and see what would happen. As the day continued at a seeming snail's pace with the heavy rain pouring down on the tin roof of my cabin, the silence I had decided to embrace so playfully and lovingly was beginning to feel like an unwelcome presence. At first, the sound of the rain, although not deafening, began to sound like a kind of heavy, monotonous engine. With time, I began to notice what seemed like a differentiation between each raindrop. And each of these raindrops started to resonate with an almost stinging presence beckoning me with each prick to allow whatever was inside of me to rise to the surface. I would say it was like a death by a thousand cuts, but it really wasn't quite that dramatic. Or maybe it was ... Nevertheless, with each passing moment, the roar of the rainstorm was like white noise in my mind—messy, undecipherable and full of stuff that I did not want to observe.

As the day dragged on, the rain insistently hammering down, I began to feel overwhelmed by the darkness that was becoming ever-present inside of me. Thoughts about the past gave rise to uncomfortable and sometimes distressing feelings. During those long hours, I ruminated on all of the mistakes I had made during the course of my life. I began to have a suffocating deluge of unworthiness, shame and despair wash over me. I resented my choice to try this "being in silence" thing and also began to experience a growing resentment for the spiritual teachers who have suggested that the practice of embracing silence can be an activity that is helpful for one's personal growth. Pushing against the discomfort and wishing that these thoughts and feelings would stop seemed to increase the unpleasantness of the whole experience. I was suffering.

Doesn't sound so delightful, does it? I had set out to practice silence in order to connect with my bliss. I wanted to feel the zenned-out luminosity

I had imagined to be possessed by the Dalai Lama, Ram Dass or Pema Chodron. Little did I know at the time, my experience was exactly what the universe had ordered. As my suffering continued, I found myself being able to allow it more and more, which was strangely surprising. I understood the practice of non-judgment with my head, but my heart was fighting against it. This was a hateful experience from which I was desperate to remove myself. Happening in a sudden and solitary moment, trying to gently breathe through tears as I sat quietly on the sofa, I unexpectedly began to let go. I questioned whether or not what I was feeling in that instant could be any worse than any negative feeling I had experienced before. After all, I was in a beautiful setting in the middle of nowhere and most notably, I was safe. I knew this, but somehow I didn't feel particularly safe and my level of discomfort was markedly among the three most uncomfortable things I had ever experienced to date. Nonetheless, I stayed with it.

SINCE WE HAVE TALKED ABOUT ALLOWING AND BEING with uncomfortable feelings often in this book, I give you this brief account not to scare you away from practicing silence but to wholeheartedly encourage you to do it. Needless to say, the feelings I spoke of before continued; until they didn't. As the rain began to subside, so did my feelings of dread and abysmal uncertainty. The stillness I was attempting to embrace, however uncomfortable it was, began to afford me the space to observe the discomfort in a way I had not done before. The silence allowed me to be a witness to the *self*, and in this silence, I began to lighten up and connect with a greater sense of peace, an all-encompassing and luminous sense of peace. The zenned-out luminosity I mentioned before never came. However, the sense of peace I am speaking of here was one of acceptance for what is and for what was. As I shifted to looking forward, my sense of calm afforded me (for the first time in my life) the capacity to look toward a future with an open heart devoid of distress, anxiety and dread. Everything I needed to move forward was already within me and it was in silence that I finally discovered that truth.

My feeling is that when we have a life where we do not acknowledge the presence of clutter, when we get run over by that figurative Mack truck with our clutter flying everywhere, instead of attending to the care of our truest self, we rush to pick up and organize all of this clutter in an attempt to make our life look or feel under control. You may or may not agree with me here, but I will say that it never works well for us to attend to the external stuff at the detriment of taking care of ourselves. I sincerely cannot stress this enough, courageous reader. This does not mean that we selfishly take care of ourselves while letting everything else go to shit. It means that we set our intention to recharge our batteries and take care of our precious self in order to have the energy and internal resources to clean up the externals—it really won't work the other way around.

So, how might your practice of silence in order to honor your truest self in this time of loss and uncertainty serve you the best? Do you need to go on a three-day retreat and create your own version of my first attempt at this practice? Probably not. What I might recommend here is something that looks more like what I do most every day.

Pause

What I would like to suggest here is for you to take on the practice of creating a pause. I am often saying to my friends and colleagues, "I just need to press the pause button for a few." Pema Chodron, a highly revered and much-loved Buddhist teacher, author and nun, speaks of silence often in her lessons. What I love about her work is that she makes taking on practices like the practice of silence accessible and, to say the very least, doable. She says that we can pause, breathe mindfully and right before our eyes, the world can open up to us. Even now in my experience, my mind can become extremely disordered as a day progresses. I can still worry about what I have failed to do, what I need to do but probably don't have time for, and what I don't feel like doing. The list can sometimes be seemingly endless and I imagine that many of you can identify with this.

BEING AWAKE ENOUGH TO REMEMBER TO "PRESS THE pause button" is like possessing a superpower. We can press the pause button while sitting at our desk or pausing in a parking lot for one minute before we go into the grocery store. If you're like me and tend to get overwhelmed at large parties or in huge groups of people, we can escape to a bathroom or some other area, shut the door and claim our one or two minutes to re-center and get grounded. Three or four slow and mindful breaths can mean the difference between having a cluttered and noisy mind or reemerging with clarity and a sense of openness. Feeling a sense of calm is a nice added benefit as well and with practice, we can access this sense of calm almost as quickly as our negative feelings arise. This is yet another way we reclaim our power.

CREATING SPACE

The practice of deliberately being in silence means that we need to create a kind of space for this silence to occur. Since many of us are relying on silence to bring us a gift of sorts, whether it be unspecified or desired, our presence can facilitate the acquisition of said gift. Our presence and ability to create a figurative space to fully hold that presence is particularly beneficial for the practice of silence.

WHAT ABOUT THE NOTION OF CREATING SPACE, NOT necessarily for the practice of silence but for affording us the opportunity to be alone with our thoughts and feelings while we process recent events? Perhaps this processing of thoughts and feelings occurs in silence but here, we are setting another arena for a different process to occur. If silence is a companion to this process, then so be it.

What I would like to speak to here is the creation of internal space and being discerning about our physical placement with regard to anything external to ourselves.

Eckhart Tolle, renowned spiritual teacher and author, speaks beautifully to the creation of space. I don't feign to fully understand everything he brings to our consciousness through his work, but the essence of what he brings is what I would like to speak to here. In his book *A New Earth*, he says that if we can connect to our inner space, the unlimited consciousness that is inherent in all of us, real happiness and the joy that is our birthright is readily available. He guides us to continue our practice of remaining awake to the quietude inside of us, embrace stillness and remain alert. All of what he says here can, of course, occur in your silence practice, but let's look at a more mundane way of connecting to our inner being as we move about our daily lives.

First, regarding our placement in relation to anything external to us (other people, public spaces, etc.), it behooves us to design an environment so that there is nothing pressing upon us or intrusive with regard to things in physical reality. This means that our surrounding physical space holds the opportunity to be highly supportive of our internal one and we can set the intention to create this space in any way we see fit. This can mean distancing ourselves from others when pursuing a deeper connection to self and this type of sequestration is not an uncommon engagement for the novice. Just a note here, we must also remain mindful of avoiding the toll that isolation can take on our well-being. Isolation for overly lengthy periods can have a negative impact on our welfare. Remember, we are creatures who not only desire connection, we require it to thrive.

As an introvert, I create space for myself throughout my day by choosing to do certain things. I intentionally construct quiet time in short periods where I am not interacting with others so that I may figuratively recharge my batteries. By the creation of this physical space, I have actively given my inner being space for an opportunity to breathe into itself, hence connecting me more deeply to who I really am. Here, separation from the noisy and busy world outside of myself is nurturing to my sense of inner peace and it only takes a small dose of this type of space to rejuvenate me. So, you can see that manipulation of anything external to ourselves by claiming physical space goes hand in hand with ensuring that our inner space is nurtured as well.

IF YOU ARE MORE EXTROVERTED, RECHARGING YOUR batteries might come from loving interaction with friends, family and even strangers. Does this mean that the extrovert need not create quiet space during times of grief while standing in the presence of uncertainty? Absolutely not. Claiming one's own version of the space I have described above is perfectly applicable for the extrovert and, in the end, necessary as well. You, dear reader, will know what is right for you.

AS WE HAVE EXPLORED ALIGNING WITH OUR ABILITY to sense our truest self and what Mr. Tolle might define as "being," how does the creation of this space work in partnership with the other tools and ideas we have explored together so far? In my estimation, the more we honor ourselves by the creation of specific activities and practices that nurture and actively ensure that we are being as loving as possible to our true self, the more we are apt to gain forward momentum toward our desire.

We move closer to the experience of thriving when we allow our self-care practices to become well integrated into the very fabric of our daily life. And who doesn't want the fabric of their life to be as cosmically fabulous as possible?

How about that?

11

Reclaiming

When it comes to bad things happening to us, we have a choice. We can rise and face our loss and uncertainty or we can collapse under the burden of our fight with those things.

There is something to be said about reclaiming a part of yourself you feel you might have lost. This sense of loss might only be connected to an internal experience or it might be directly related to a place existing in physical reality. A tender and cherished memory might be wrapped up in the place itself, waiting for you to reclaim it. Nothing has essentially been lost here, but our current level of suffering with regard to what we are facing can indeed feel as though an integral part of who we are has vanished. With the sense of uncertainty we are facing, loss is a most certain sidekick, however unwelcome. Taking back the luminous energy of an experience or place you once held with fondness can be a way of reclaiming that the memory and the place still hold a loving presence for us. This loving presence is truly not diminished even if the memory is marked by the rough edges of sorrow or is seemingly smothered by a deep sense of loss.

WHEN THE PAST COMES TO MEET US WITH MEMORIES rising up surrounding the relationship we once cherished that has now ended or is in limbo, sometimes elicited by a Facebook post or through a conversation with a friend, we might feel a rush of sadness descend upon us. Sitting with this memory or visiting a place we shared with the one we loved so deeply might be difficult. Since the former affection we once connected with this place or memory activated feelings of delight or even bliss, encountering it again can now be painful. We might find that the sweetness we once had that was associated with the place or memory has dissipated and now we are left with a barren and empty void inside of us.

ONE AFTERNOON, WHEN SPEAKING WITH A DEAR friend, I was recounting a story about visiting

London during my transition back home and how I had returned to some places my spouse and I had visited together on our honeymoon. The adventure into reclaiming these places began on my flight over to London. Somewhere over the Atlantic, I started feeling sadness and flutters of worry rising up in me. I worried that if I visited these places again, I would be overcome with feelings of grief and loss. I also wondered how painful these might be, if I could hold them with openness and if I should even consider playing in that sandbox, so to speak.

SITTING WITH THESE THOUGHTS IN SILENCE AS THE plane made its way across the Atlantic, I set my intention to reclaim the places and the memories associated with them as my own. During our honeymoon stay in London, I took my spouse to several spots that held great meaning for me. I had lived there for a number of years in the '90s and had frequented these places, bringing friends and family members there so they could share the experience with me. Upon my arrival, I set out to spend time in my favorite spot in all of London, Hampstead Heath. It is a magical place where you can forget that you are even in a city—pretty extraordinary for a city the size of London! Kenwood House, a stately, seventeenth-century manor now open to the public, sits majestically overlooking an area of lawn and forest. Within its confines is a wonderful restaurant / tea shop that serves delightful English fare in an idyllic setting that is not only beautiful but somehow comforting and fills me with serenity.

As I sat in the lovely garden enjoying a plateful of sandwiches, two types of cake and multiple pots of Earl Grey tea, I thought to myself, "This place was mine first. I've shared it with many people I love and the experience of sharing it with my spouse was luminous and worthy of acknowledgment." Rather than colluding with the negative thoughts that sought to rise up about how this place might be spoiled now, I chose to sit and be present with the beauty that was all around me and remind myself that in spite of everything that had happened, this place was somehow still mine. It was in this moment that I realized I had reclaimed it and it became clear that absolutely nothing had been taken away from me or the inherent magic that is Kenwood House and Hampstead Heath. Spacious is the only way I could describe my inner state in that moment and this spaciousness was a welcome surprise.

. . .

I CONTINUED THIS LITTLE THOUGHT EXPERIMENT OF mine with other locations in London and Italy. What I discovered in these places was that I had a choice regarding what to hold while visiting them. I asked myself to discern what I truly wanted from these memorable spots. Did I want my memory of them to be laden with the darkness of resentment and an immensity of sadness? Or did I wish to rejuvenate my experience of them by remaining open to the possibility that I possessed the power to give them the meaning of my choice? So, courageous reader, do you know what I chose to be present to? All of it. Yes, I set my intention to be with the sadness and heavy tug of loss while remaining open and accepting of the presence of love: love for the places, openhearted regard for the love that was experienced there in the past and the love that I carried with me in the present moment. There was an abundance of it! Love was and is ever-present.

CAN YOU SEE HOW TURNING AWAY FROM THE LOVE that was permeating these places (and is always present everywhere if you are still with me) would have served no purpose except give rise to self-created suffering? I had somehow known that I would have some access to the kind of deeply loving experience I'm talking about here. However, I did not think it would become an all-encompassing one as I made my way to all of these spots that I loved so dearly. It was a full-body experience and there was no denying the presence of something that, dare I say it, gave me the warm fuzzies. Yep, I said it. Love, the presence of it, gives me the warm fuzzies and I want to have the warm fuzzies in abundance!

THERE WAS MOMENTUM IN ALL OF THIS AND AS I began to feel more connected to Love rather than regret, my heart chose to be with Love rather than despair. I chose to be with the momentum of the easily accessible thing that made me feel good, Love. I connected with the radiance emanating from within me and simply stayed there. Once I acknowledged Love and sank into the warm embrace of loving presence, it was effortless for me to set my intention to be present. I did not collude with the negative stories I had previously held about the past and stopped being concerned about the future. I comfortably slid into the present moment, was fully embraced by it and there I remained. No effort, only ease and the presence of grace. Remember her? She always gives the best hugs ...

. . .

So, I HAVE TO SAY HERE THAT THE PROCESS OF reclaiming these spaces wrapped in fond memories contained more curious discovery for me than I was expecting. The very linear way my brain normally functions had me believing that the ritual of attending to these memories and places would culminate in a neatly arranged, bullet point list of achievements, things I had conquered. But this wasn't the case. Allowing myself to discover what fruits I would take away from this experience by simply being present to where I was in any given moment provided me with an end result that was surprising, to say the least. This type of presence included attending to what was happening internally and setting my intention to be with everything externally as well. In the end, there was no neatly compiled list. There were no achievements to acknowledge. There was only the recognition that everything was just as it should be and I understood that I didn't have to do anything or try to figure out anything. I felt a deep sense of gratitude for the presence of well-being and its embrace. And not unlike the warmth of a good cup of tea, a blanket in front of a good fire on a winter's evening or that hug from Grace that I mentioned before, loving presence has and will always be the one thing that returns me to me.

. . .

ODDLY ENOUGH, THERE WAS GREAT POWER IN THESE experiences, even the really difficult ones. With a deep knowing, I understood that I had recovered some of my power, not by controlling, arranging or organizing but by allowing. Again, this was a huge surprise for me.

You

And then there is you, courageous one, reading these words and perhaps having questions arise about your own process and how you might embrace your version of the experiences I am speaking of here. Do you wish to reclaim ownership of some of your fond memories and perhaps even reclaim a place that holds great meaning for you? As you begin to look inward and observe the memories and places you wish to revisit, take a breath and check out your internal landscape. What feels splintered? What feels lost? Remember this: What feels lost or splintered is not necessarily lost or splintered. The experience of these things might feel lost or splintered, but the truth might be that the resonance of these is fuller. Think about this: Things may feel splintered simply because we are hurting and in pain, so acknowledge the pain and remember that there is nothing wrong with feeling this way. Feeling this way means that you are beautifully human and if we are able to frame this experience as being "rich" rather than being filled with deficits, then we have found a kind of mastery that few will ever sustain.

Just as ice cream makes us feel "good," and loss and uncertainty make us feel "bad," what if the simple act of reframing the way we see these things can shift our current experience from a "bad" one to at the very least a bearable one? Notice the quotes around the words "good" and "bad." If you can find a place in your heart and mind that recognizes that there really is no "good" or "bad" but that everything simply is, then perhaps your level of suffering might decrease. I will remind you again that we all have the capacity to learn how to hold all of the things that trouble us in a hugely expansive way. We simply must be gentle with ourselves when embarking on this type of self-study.

Making even the tiniest shift here can be the starting point for a new awareness to sprout from the seedbed you have so lovingly planted. You, my sweet, courageous reader, have planted this seedbed well. You have come on this journey with me and have already affected positive change in your being purely by staying the course with reading this book. Now that you are ready to reclaim whatever it is that will have you resting in your seat of power, take a breath, look forward, and let's head on to the next part of our adventure.

12

On the Ground: Let Your Environment Coach You

When it comes to integrating life's lessons,
we get to choose which ones we will learn from.
Why not choose them all?

Y ou might be finding it difficult these days to find yourself on the ground. You might now be wondering what I mean by the phrase "on the ground?" Being on the ground means having the experience of being grounded, centered, and slipping into stillness with ease. Being in contact with your *self* in a way that the external environment doesn't intrude upon or invade that connection to self is a primary element of being on the ground. Before I go on, I have to bust myself and say that my inherent nature has never afforded me any ease when it comes to being "on the ground." That being said, I have had practices for many years that keep me on the ground, but I will be frank in saying that during the experience that led me to write this book, I sometimes found it difficult to feel truly grounded. My innate tendency is to run on the anxious side and over the course of my life, I was politely referred to as "highly strung." That truly makes me laugh! Sometimes my idiosyncrasies got the better of me when I was younger. I have my moments now, but they pale in comparison to the wild emotional rides I used to take. However, I am human and I recognize that the struggle to stay on the ground can be a real experience for anyone, especially when we are faced with an event like discovering that our partner has cheated.

IF YOU HAVE BEEN READING THIS BOOK IN A LINEAR way, you know that I have been talking quite a bit about being centered. I find it very interesting how adverse life experiences can bring us new perspectives about the things we are currently holding in the present moment. We think we have a handle on how things are or should be and then we are challenged by some life event that shakes us to the core. Bam! We suddenly have a new worldview that is unexpected, sometimes unwelcome, yet nevertheless, enlightening. Also, if we are awake and receptive to everything in our immediate vicinity, including the people, places and things we encounter, there is a wealth of information right before us, ready to coach us. And this, dear reader, leads me to the notion of being coached by our environment.

Scottish folk

I began writing this chapter at the start of my living in Scotland and it was my experience with the Scottish people, two very good friends and some new ones who appeared on my path in particular, that I found myself observing something that I might classify as a cultural difference as compared to my own upbringing in the United States. Hanging around with Scottish people sparked my use of the phrase "on the ground" and one individual I met early on while living in the country embodied the very definition of that phrase in their way of being on a day-to-day basis. This person, although sensitive and very in touch with their spiritual center and emotions, possessed what seemed to be an inherent capacity for staying on the ground even in moments when emotions might run on the high end of the spectrum. The practicality of getting on with it with a kind of stoic pragmatism seemed to come with ease—it was an inherent trait that was ever-present. Sure, they still presented with a full range of emotions and the capacity to be flustered like any other human, but they engaged these shifts with seemingly lead-filled boots. I witnessed different versions of this in many other people as well, but this person who was acutely present to my experience had something that I wanted and I wished that it would come as easily to me as it seemed to come to them. However, it really isn't about how easy the skill set comes; it's just about having the skill set to whatever degree one develops it. Also, overdevelopment of this skill set can mean that we deflect or suppress negative emotions without allowing them to simply be what they are: a fleeting experience that is not indicative of who we really are.

ANOTHER IMPORTANT ELEMENT TO REMEMBER IS that we cannot be so focused on being grounded that we lose flexibility. If we become rigid in our way of being in order to exert control over our environment both internally and externally in some askew attempt to feel grounded, we risk becoming closed to new perspectives and experiences. Human relationships are the playground for learning and engaging the experience of being open to new ideas. They are the figurative petri dish where we develop a skill set for considering someone else's opinion and meeting them where they are even though the opinions may be in direct opposition to one another. Sometimes these interactions are unsettling and challenge our preconceived ideas about who we are. We often want to be right, and proving that we are right does not at all indicate that we are on the ground, no matter how much we want it to be the determining factor. Difficult interactions where our emotions become heightened can have us feeling like the ground has disappeared from underneath us. This does not necessarily mean we are coming apart or actually losing our contact with the ground. It simply indicates we have engaged our courage and vulnerability. The novel experience of absorbing new insight in the aftermath of the challenging interaction may mean that growth is at hand if we are open and flexible. Taking on a new perspective could be just what we need, and by integrating that experience, believe it or not, our capacity for being grounded has increased.

MAKING THE SHIFT FROM FEELING RATTLED BY acute or heightened emotions and turning one's attention to the more strengths-focused outlook of getting steady and getting on with it is an ability anyone can develop. This shift in attention is not about deflecting, suppressing or ignoring the emotional undercurrent at hand; it is more about regaining momentum while holding all of it—the entire experience. We discover that the difficult emotional experience continues to be honored while we turn our attention toward a more productive use of our energy. Holding this polarity means we can have the experience of gaining forward momentum rather than being stuck neck-deep in the discomfort. The feeling of discomfort is more than likely still there, but it does not own the entire space where the experience resides.

I HAVE STARTED TO WONDER IF WE SOMETIMES overthink all of these ideas instead of connecting deeply to something that is fundamentally ours. For thousands of years, we didn't have therapists or coaches as we define them today. We had spiritual leaders, masters, guides and wisdom holders in our tribes and I imagine that if we had not possessed the inherent ability to get on the ground, not unlike the way we are observing here, we would have ceased to exist. I have stated before that all of us are whole and complete, and stealing language directly from my former spouse, we have our own answers.

If we decode that we will engage from this premise and integrate it as part of our belief system, we can begin to rest in full acceptance of our wholeness and completeness while trusting that the answers we seek are already present within us. That sounds like a nice balance between head and heart, and that's a good thing.

LET ME SAY THIS. WE ARE NOT LOOKING TO NEGATE the value of the very human experience of being off the ground simply because we are focusing on being grounded. Feeling ungrounded is normal and much needed in our experience as human beings since being "off the ground" is the place from which we learn many lessons. It is in these contrasting moments that we find great wisdom presented to us if we are awake enough and willing enough to receive it. Most likely, feeling or being grounded through a difficult experience like the one we are exploring in this book is a common desire for anyone facing this type of loss.

SO, ONCE AGAIN, ONE QUESTION WE MUST ASK ourselves is, "How do we shift back to the place where we find ourselves centered, on the ground and continue to move forward while honoring the contrast and discomfort we might be feeling?" There are all kinds of teachings out there about grounding and centering and therapists find themselves bringing grounding and centering techniques to those in distress, often on an almost daily basis. Coaches often bring these practices into the work where clients may be experiencing forward momentum but need to re-center and refocus. This type of grounding can afford the client a springboard for shaking free from the feeling of being stuck and lay a path for returning to forward momentum. Nevertheless, developing the skill set for quickly shifting to a place where we are once again on the ground is one that can be established by anyone. Perhaps the experiences of our early environment never coached us to be on the ground, which for some can mean that being centered during challenging times is difficult, to say the least. As I mentioned before, it seems that the people of Scotland seemingly have this ability for free. Yes, I am making a sweeping and overly generalized statement here, but this characteristic is a common thread running through the entirety of the culture and I feel fortunate enough to witness this firsthand on a daily basis.

. . .

THE BIGGER QUESTION I WOULD LIKE TO HOLD HERE is, "What do we notice from our environment and surroundings that can coach us to find the balance and experience of being grounded that we are seeking?"

FOR A START, LOOK AROUND YOU. WHO ARE THE people who always seem steady, or even better, remain grounded when the going gets tough? What do you notice about them? Do they have traits that you wish you inherently possessed? Can you pinpoint identifying properties of these traits and find them within yourself? If you have difficulty finding them within, what are some of the elements that you would like to cultivate from scratch upon observation of others? Whether we discover these elements residing deep within our own internal resources or we set our intention to develop a fresh skill that we know will benefit how we show up in the world, finding our own unique way of getting on the ground can do nothing but afford us greater well-being. Full stop.

OH, MY SHINY, HAPPY, COURAGEOUS READER, WHAT is your next step? Will you bring a conversation about grounding to your therapist or coach? Will you go and read some literature on developing a skill set for being grounded during difficult times? I encourage you to engage other people's stories on social media and search through articles easily found on the Internet addressing this topic. When you find wisdom that is easy for you to integrate and put into practice, remember to note that the very act of seeking will have shifted you to a place of feeling more on the ground. Take those skills, integrate them further into your being and grounded you will surely be.

From that place, anything is possible.

13

Intention

"*I learned this, at least, by my experiment; that if one advances confidently in the direction of his dreams, and endeavors to live the life which he has imagined, he will meet with a success unexpected in common hours.*"
—Henry David Thoreau

THE QUOTE AT THE START OF THIS CHAPTER WAS SO resonant with the intention of this chapter that I simply had to use it. Setting our intention is one of the most mindful and powerful activities we can perform. When we set our intention, we turn an energetic thought form into reality. We might even verbalize this intention to give it vibration. We might solidify this intention by writing it down and posting it somewhere so we will be reminded of how we are assigning direction to our course.

Setting our intention means we are declaring to the universe what it is that we intend to make manifest, and since the part of the brain where we set intention is located at the front of our skull, I like to say that we really are leading with our head. This is undoubtedly a mindful activity since our frontal cortex is the place in the brain where we make decisions and engage our follow-through optimistically with the most lucidity we can muster.

AT THIS TIME OF UNCERTAINTY, WHEN FACING THE aftermath of a cheater, we might find some difficulty setting our intention since our world has seemingly been blown apart. There are all kinds of distractions, both internal and external, that can carry us off track. Our world hasn't literally been blown apart, but it probably feels like it for most who have had the experience of discovering a cheating spouse. Decision-making processes might be muddled by the presence of racing and intrusive thoughts, unanswered questions and the unrelenting pace of the world around us. It's all clutter and the lists of diversions go on and on for most of us. Think back on what we explored about clutter in the chapter "Silence and Creating Space": it is entirely up to us to wipe out the clutter in order to find clarity.

So, HOW DO WE, IN THE MOST MINDFUL WAY AND with the most clarity we can gather, set our intention? As I mentioned before, it might not seem so easy in this moment. However, if we allow some space for Grace to be present and bring in a bit of ease by keeping it simple, we might find that intention setting is the easy part. Making space for the setting of our intention might take a little more effort, but if we are willing, that willingness can be the main element for clearing a path to the way forward.

I IMAGINE MOST OF US HAVE THE EXPERIENCE OF facing multiple factors outside of ourselves that pull at our sense of presence. Some of these external factors we signed up for and some we didn't. We have jobs, children, and pets. We have friends and family members with whom we regularly interact or with whom we are expected to interact. We have bills to pay, deadlines, to-do lists and again, the list goes on and on. There are stressors present we didn't ask for as well: bad news on the television, an ill or dying family member, our car breaks down, winter is coming and we have seasonal affective disorder ... I am sure by now you get the picture.

. . .

IN THE CHAPTER "SILENCE AND CREATING SPACE," I speak to the notion of creating a pause when we feel called to do so. It is in this pause where we find a deeper connection to our truest self. What might it be like to take this pause and simply make it about organizing our "space," both internal and external, so that there exists a metaphoric place where we can set our intention with the utmost clarity and minimal distractions? I will tell you right now that the space I am speaking of does not require a figurative bulldozer to clear it, nor does it require a huge amount of time set aside for this space to work well for you to give you the breathing room you desire for this intention setting step.

IF YOU ARE FINDING IT DIFFICULT TO DETERMINE where to begin this process and have not yet found the space you need to be with your intention setting, try carrying around a notepad or use the note-taking feature on your phone, and whenever you have a possible intention come to mind, jot it down. You can do this anytime throughout the day, or if you are like me, ideas come in the middle of the night or some other time or place that doesn't seem to fit the typical arena for intention setting. Ideas

Intentions are not set in stone. If we are driven, urging forward without being aware of our surroundings, we can miss a figurative road sign telling us that we need to course correct. Course correction is an integral element of any type of life process, and as soon as we solidify that our intention must be exactly what we set forth from the start with absolutely no deviation, we diminish the possibility of having the richest experience available to us.

Since we are in the throes of a particularly difficult situation, intention setting while remaining flexible means that we can connect to our capacity for remaining open to whatever life brings to our path. These are uncertain and challenging times, courageous reader. By now, you have learned that the more rigid and driven we are, the less apt we are to stay in alignment with who we really are. It is in this moment that we remind ourselves of our standards of integrity and think of them as fundamental parts of a compass for which we divine the connection to our true self.

Uncertainty and intentions

Uncertainty is often experienced as a disruptor

for a clear path. So, dear reader, how do we navigate a path that seems unclear with the fog of uncertainty obstructing our vision? Since we know that life is truly made up of a series of cycles and different types of growth, however uncomfortable, can we allow ourselves to embrace the uncertainty rather than fight it? Can we set our intention in spite of an unclear path before us? Feelings of doubt, disorientation and anxiety are common during times like these. If we stay with the idea that everything passes, even the heavy fog of uncertainty, then perhaps we can be gentle with ourselves when setting our intentions. Remember, we are looking for forward momentum and it only takes a tiny nudge in the right direction for that forward momentum to begin. Right now, we are growing in an exponential way since we have decided that curious self-study in this harrowing moment is the only way forward. We are looking to find our rhythm, our groove and again, we are being called upon to allow the presence of Grace, call forth our capacity for acceptance and with the brightest spark our minds can generate, we set our intention to once again step forward on our path. Courageous. Bold. Unapologetic.

. . .

SETTING OUR INTENTION IN TIMES THAT ARE DARK and filled with doubt has got to be one of the most courageous acts that we engage as human beings. It is definitely a bold act since many of us have the experience of being completely unprepared for even the most benign occurrence that transpires on our path as we are experiencing deep uncertainty. I mention the element of setting our intentions in an unapologetic way for two reasons. The first reason is that our monkey mind can get in the way of our intention setting since it wants us to play small in this arena. It is simply attempting to keep us safe, but truthfully, it is not serving us here. The second reason is that other people's monkey minds can become intrusive to our experience since often-times, they too would like us to play small. Again, perhaps they want us to be safe and I will state it again: playing safe in moments like these tends to keep us treading water or hanging out knee-deep in the muck of the experience we are having rather than gaining that forward momentum we so desire.

AND NOW, WHAT IS YOUR FIRST STEP? WILL YOU SET smaller intentions that inherently have doable outcomes so that forward momentum is experienced in an organic yet visceral way? Will you set some larger intentions then break these intentions down into doable elements? The truth is, there is no set formula so remember, flexibility is your friend, course correcting still has the element of forward momentum and being gentle with yourself means that the battery pack required to complete this mission remains fully charged.

I LOVE YOU.

14

Falling Off the Wagon

The only way to gain forward momentum
is to get up and get moving.

I have learned how to face-plant, get back up again, dust myself off and keep moving forward. For a lot of my life, I would face-plant and lie in the mud kvetching about the miserable state of my existence. Face-planting is something I will probably always do since I tend to run on the clumsy side both physically and, yes, psychologically and emotionally. I am human after all. The difference now is that I am able to rise figuratively covered in mud and move forward with my head held high. Well, more often than I used to. It's a nice feeling and it only took some forty-odd years to get to where I am with that. Again, to be human ...

· · ·

THE THING ABOUT THE WORK THAT WE ARE exploring in this book is that all of us can fall off the wagon with regard to our practices that keep us mindful and centered. Our real job in these moments, when we do fall off this figurative wagon, is to return to mindful presence, stop the judgment and stand back up so we can regain forward momentum and get back into our flow state.

SO, HERE IS MY FALLING OFF THE WAGON STORY THAT happened while writing this book. For months I had been methodical in my practices for maintaining balance and well-being. I was exercising, eating extremely well and had lost fifteen pounds without even being concerned with losing fifteen pounds. Side note: I needed to lose this weight as I was feeling sluggish and unhealthy and it was only as the weight came off that I began to notice a renewed vitality in my everyday experience. I recaptured feeling really good about my body and self-image. This positive sense of self had eluded me for a few weeks after learning that my spouse had cheated. Doubts surfaced about my attractiveness and ability to hold someone's interest sexually. I felt ugly and undesirable and with these feelings came shame and a sense of unworthiness, but I digress.

· · ·

After these few weeks of feeling sorry for myself, I set my intention to settle into the practices we have explored in this book. These practices combined with other self-care elements while setting daily intentions to BE in alignment with my best self meant that I once again began to truly feel like my best self. Until one day, I didn't.

There came a day almost five months into this journey when I woke up after a terribly restless night with racing thoughts and the weedy sprouts of rumination on resentments I had never fully addressed, beginning to fill the self-care seedbed I had so lovingly created. I relinquished the power I had tapped into when I planted this seedbed by colluding with the anger that had not yet fully dissipated from my mind and heart. Instead of mindfully turning my attention away from those thoughts and reconnecting with my true self, I hung around in that space. It was kind of like willingly rolling around in a poop-filled sandbox, a sandbox I had created, pooped in and was not awake enough to clean up or even leave. I was purposely fighting with the experience rather than allowing it to simply be what it was. Two days later, after sleepless nights and days spent in the dirty sandbox, angry and unwilling to budge, I ended up with my first case of shingles.

I HAD HEARD ABOUT THIS CONDITION AND THE stories had always given me the fear! And if you have never had shingles but have heard the stories, yes, they are as bad as you have heard and probably worse than you can actually imagine. At least that was my experience. The morning of that third day, I assumed I had been bitten by something and the rash that had appeared had me racing to the doctor in my small town in Italy after receiving some advice from a couple of friends.

THE DOCTOR ASKED ME IF I HAD EXPERIENCED ANY level of stress and if I had been sleeping well. Of course, my answers to these questions were "yes" and "no." Within that same day, as the condition progressed, the entire right side of my body looked like someone had doused me with some sort of caustic substance. Blisters appeared and began to burn and throb with pain—I was suffering, to say the least. Not only was my body suffering in direct response to the suffering I had created in my mind, but my spirit was diminished and the connection to my true self was thin and wavering.

I HAD FALLEN OFF THE WAGON AND IN THE THROES of this physical suffering, I somehow woke up. I felt and still feel to this day immensely grateful for the experience of my beautiful, attuned body to alert me to the fact I had shifted out of alignment with who I really am. Over the next two weeks, the painful condition was unrelenting in its attack on my comfort level. Daily, I was bombarded with a physical pain unlike anything I had ever experienced and through it all, I was able to find a sense of gratitude and even a smattering of calm while I grounded myself and got on with the writing of this book. I visited close friends in Scotland and was able to remain present to their love and support even through the pain—the pain of the physical condition as well as the ongoing pain of loss and grief. I was once again allowing all of it to be present without fighting it, even the physical pain.

IT WOULD BE VERY EASY AND VERY HUMAN OF ME TO look back on this experience with some amount of judgment. I could say, "Look what I did myself! How awful!" But I wonder how taking that perspective might have served me as I moved forward? Isn't the very nature of looking at the past with a figurative truckload of judgment the thing that keeps us out of the present? Is it possible that if I hang out in that type of energy again that I might start the momentum of negative thoughts and feelings that could once again lead to some amount of the physical, psychological and spiritual suffering? Quite possibly and most likely, the answer to all of these questions is, "Yes." And if that is the answer, why would I ever want to create that kind of suffering again, especially when I know better and when I know I inherently possess the power to shift my perspective, tap into my best self and keep the suffering to a minimum? As we have explored before, suffering will always be present, but why create more of it when we know just how *not* to do that?

So, as I said before, I have become quite adept at face-planting, getting back up in whatever level of composure and moving forward. Earlier I spoke of waking up in the throes of all of this suffering. How is it that I actually woke up in that moment, you might ask? For most of us, or at least many of us, having a lightbulb moment when things are a shit show it's probably not a common occurrence. Most of the time in my life, especially during the darkest moments, they basically stayed dark. So again, what was different about this moment?

WHEN WE SPEND TIME STUDYING OURSELVES, learning about what makes us tick and thinking about how we apply skills we develop to our experience with the world around us, somehow the brain has a lot better chance at waking us up in these dark moments than it does when we do no type of self-study. You know by now, courageous reader, that you have been engaging in a type of self-study that is probably putting a polish on the lens through which you view the world around you. The more you engage in this type of study, the quicker you will wake up and you will sometimes, with the presence of Grace, wake up in your darkest moments. It really is as simple as that. Do nothing, stay asleep. Continue to do the thing we are doing together throughout the course of this book, be a rock star.

HOW ABOUT THAT?

15

Looking Forward

When we think it's all over, it's really just the beginning.

With all of the uncertainty that happens at the beginning of a breakup, there comes a time when we know that the relationship, the one we have treasured so dearly, is truly over. I say "over," meaning that what we once understood that relationship to be and how we defined it has ended. So, what if something else is beginning to happen with this relationship, perhaps a shift or a course correction? If you have continued to communicate and be present to one another, maybe that relationship is evolving into something else.

· · ·

At the beginning of this experience, I mistakenly imagined that severing all ties would be the "trick" for maintaining my sanity and reclaiming my power. I was fully convinced that with this severance, I would feel better and be able to move forward in a more positive way while walking my life path. For some time, I entertained the idea of going completely solo without any further connection to my spouse. What I noticed about my experience was that I felt a deep and unrelenting sense of emptiness that was pervasive, leaving me feeling disconnected from my truest self. So, instead of allowing a flight response to be the driver of my behavior and actions, I chose to be present to what was happening and turn my attention away from ruminating on the past or worrying about the future. This was intensely hard work for me. It took some time, but in the end, it was through this endeavor that I found another kind of connection with my former spouse since I had created a kind of internal space for my willingness to be present, which in turn allowed their spark of divinity to also be present to mine. I did not wish to engage in a relationship where we would connect on a new level, but I did have an understanding that severing all ties and disconnecting in the way I described before meant that I would not be allowing the presence of Love to stand with me or with us for that matter.

For a time, our relationship became even more loving, which was a complete and total surprise to me since I was fully convinced that any kind of loving interaction would never be possible again. Through this, I shifted to being in a more brutally honest place, not only with my former spouse but with myself. My needs moved to the forefront of my mind and heart and I made sure, first and foremost, that I was transparent with my thoughts and feelings. I endeavored to shield nothing from coming into my experience since I felt it was my prerogative to do so and that allowing all of it meant a richer experience was at hand. This, in turn, bolstered my sense of power and again, this was a total surprise for me.

Somehow, I was awake enough to realize that if I continued to hold resentment in my heart and trudge forward without releasing the bitterness that was beginning to permeate my entire experience, that bitterness would be a burden of my own creation that I would carry with me and the responsibility for that burden was solely my own. I did not want any of that self-created suffering. When I chose to be present to what was happening in that moment, I discovered that the presence of Love was brighter than any kind of anger that was still lingering. In the end, all of it can be distilled right down to the practices I have spoken about in this book. Was I truly able to be curious, open, accepting and loving in the face of loss and uncertainty? You might remember the tool COAL from the chapter "Looking Back." Also, my practice included the elements from RAIN, a tool we examined in the chapter "Out of the Darkness." Could I recognize what was happening, allow it to simply be what it was, investigate it lovingly and then mindfully move away from identifying with it? This was complex and tricky work for me, but somehow, grace kept me buoyant and willing to do the work.

I'VE SPOKEN TO MANY PEOPLE WHO HAVE MANAGED to maintain a positive connection with the one with whom they were partnered by allowing friendship and continued relationship to blossom through loving interactions. This might be a real challenge for some, and for others, it might come more easily. Nevertheless, if you are seeking to align with your best self, you might ask yourself the question, "Who am I willing to be throughout this experience?" If you are choosing an open and accepting heart, the presence of Love will guide you—I am certain of that. This is not to say that for the shift in this experience to be fruitful that we must maintain some kind of connection with someone who abandoned us. We might choose that completely disconnecting is the cleanest and most healthy path we can take. For others, ongoing communication and loving presence while finding a different type of connection are possible. For a while, my former spouse and I were able to maintain a relationship with one another that was kind, albeit businesslike. I think we both did our best to bring a loving presence to our interactions and I was able to disconnect from that relationship in moments without shame or blame since I was resting fully in my sense of worth—if I didn't want any kind of interaction, then we didn't have one and my former spouse respected that. This type of boundary setting might not come easily to some, nor is it needed in some cases. However, the gift occurred in having the experience of fully addressing my needs unapologetically. That, courageous reader, was a revelation. Even though I had years of self-study lifting me up in this moment, I was still surprised that old schemas didn't take a firmer hold.

. . .

IT WAS MY EXPERIENCE THAT USING THE aforementioned tools, COAL and RAIN, was somewhat like a cure-all for what might be ailing me at any given time during the early days of this unwelcome experience. I decided that the creation of my own suffering through holding on to past resentments and worrying about the future was not an activity I wanted to engage in for any amount of time. Engaging the practice of acceptance and turning this practice toward what was happening for me in the present moment meant that setting my intention to stand with this painful experience while at the same time being filled with a sense of hopelessness was an invitation for my best self to emerge and get in the driver seat. My true self simply had to show up in this moment. As we've talked about before, when we lean into these feelings and thoughts and do not flee from them or fight them, they diminish. This has happened in my experience and it has also been reported by the many clients I have coached or to whom I have provided therapeutic guidance.

IF YOU COME THIS FAR AND ARE STILL HAVING A hard time sensing, feeling and believing the principles we have explored here, I will suggest, as I have done before, that you put the book down, hide it away somewhere and take a pause lasting a day or two, a couple of weeks or a couple of months, however long you need. Return here when you are ready—you will intuitively know when the time is right for more of this kind of self-study. Come back to this work with your innate sense of curiosity fully primed. Ask yourself the question, "Might there truly be a key to my feeling good again in any of this?" Try saying to yourself, "Is there anything to be lost by my exploring some of these ideas again? Just because I wasn't ready in the beginning doesn't mean that I'm not ready now." Also, if you have come this far with me, you have probably figured out that the real goal of this book is not to help you try and figure out how to do this thing called a breakup or a divorce, and so on. This book is really about connecting with who you really are while accessing your innate gifts that afford you the ability to diminish your suffering. Perhaps even more importantly, this book is about how to be with your pain while moving forward with a loving and coura-geous heart. You have the ability to reclaim your power and bring forth your luminosity through loving attendance to your truest self. Everything you think you need you already possess on the inside of you since the thing that will lift you is the essence of which you are made—love.

. . .

I HAVE SAID IT AGAIN AND AGAIN IN THIS BOOK AND I am going to say it here one last time. Be gentle with yourself, courageous one, BE gentle. Remember that since you are made of love, the presence of love is always with you. You are loved more fully than you can ever imagine and if you can imagine it, then all the better for you and all the better for everyone with whom you come in contact since the light you inherently possess will always be present no matter what. And because you have set your intention to tap into this light and have made the choice to have it be part of your daily experience, only good can follow since you will be bringing your best self to every experience from here on out—the joyous ones, the painful ones, all of them.

IN THE AFTERMATH OF THIS PAINFUL EVENT, IF YOU have chosen to follow some of the guidance we have explored thus far, perhaps you will reflect upon the richness of this experience rather than viewing it with a lens tainted with lack. We get to choose the quality of our life and that quality is interdependent with what happens outside of us. In the end, where we place our attention will determine the quality of our experience. We can choose to perpetually ruminate on the difficulties and hardships we have endured or we can simply be with the luminous moments that happened throughout. Yes, there were difficult moments and these difficult moments must be honored. However, these moments can sometimes take hold of our entire view. I will remind you that there were also moments filled with light. So, in this moment, if you are given the choice to hang out in the light or isolate yourself in the dark, which will you choose?

WHAT REMAINS HERE IS THE TRUTH THAT WHATEVER you decide regarding your relationship with the one who cheated, whatever choice you make, will be fully resonant with your current experience and will be in full alignment with your greater good. You see, you have come this far on this journey, continuing to challenge yourself, continuing to grow and allowing your experience to simply be what it is.

WELL DONE.

16

Contribution: Getting Outside Yourself

"If it doesn't challenge you, it doesn't change you."
—Anonymous

etting outside myself has never been particularly easy for me. When I was younger, my tendency was to become peevish and hang around sluggishly in self-created suffering. Negative thoughts and emotions often took over and became a heavy weight that I lugged around at length. My inherent tendency is to go inward but not always in a positive way like some of the ways we have explored in this book. It is one thing to set our intention for self-study and exploration in quietude while plumbing the depths of our self and quite another to expedite a spiral into the depths of our darkness in isolation, asleep to the fact that we are creating our own suffering. Rumination is the enemy here and we must be vigilant observers of our own tendencies as well as track for new behaviours that might exacerbate our already difficult time. One thing I know for sure is that when we have allowed the momentum of that spiral to happen in a mindless way, we often find ourselves at the bottom of a figurative hole we have dug and it can be difficult to climb out. The walls are slippery, muddy and searching for something in the dark to hang on to can feel like a fruitless occupation. The more we hang out there, the darker it can get, or so it might seem. It all depends upon our perspective, and if we have the skill set to shift that perspective toward the truth, away from the clutter that our mind hurls upon us, we can rise to the surface and stand in the light.

WHAT IS NECESSARY FOR US TO REACH THE SURFACE and step back into a clearer sense of self? Is it the power of positive thinking? I tend to be cynical when it comes to a meme like this one since in the end, it really is just a meme and, in my opinion, it is a destructive one. Along with it comes the accompanying baggage of shame for those who can't seem to find a way into a positive mindset. Positive thinking can't be turned on like a light switch, although there are many out there who would proclaim that a shift into positivity is as simple as pivoting on the spot. There is of course nothing simple about this process, yet perhaps there is a way to make a shift toward alignment with our true self with some facility once we have developed the skill. The positivity may or may not come. If we are mindfully observing our experience, then we might realize that the presence of positivity or lack thereof simply is what it is.

We have talked a lot about setting our intention to allow the presence of a painful experience to merely be a painful experience and nothing more. And after we have lovingly spent time with all of that uncomfortable material in the most present and mindful state we can muster, what next? Don't we all desire the radiant experience of standing in the light and feeling ourselves thrive in the face of anything currently happening in our lives—the good, the bad, and even the undefinable?

If you have found that while reading this book you have felt a connection to your sense of purpose and perhaps, even more importantly, an understanding of how you take that purpose and turn it into a contribution, then maybe the understanding of that contribution and how it occurs in physical reality is the one thing that might help you build a ladder to climb out of that figurative hole we mentioned earlier. I know that when my negative emotions are heavy and seemingly overpowering, turning my attention to what I know I am here to do in the world provides me with some provender for taking authentic action. During the course of writing this book, I found myself in the figurative hole I had dug more times than I can count. What got me outside of myself was the activity of sitting down and putting words on paper, or rather, my Mac, as it just so happens.

EVEN WHEN I FOUND MYSELF FEELING DEVOID OF inspiration with my mind working in overdrive to tell me that I had no business writing this book, I was nevertheless able to connect to my willingness. I was willing to engage in the activity of writing. I was willing to set my intention to take two hours, write whatever came to me and toss aside judgment even if the only thing I came up with was five paragraphs. Sometimes I consciously did the thing I had set out to do even if I didn't feel like it.

. . .

I SHARE THIS WITH YOU, COURAGEOUS ONE, SINCE on more than one occasion, I surprised myself. Have you ever done a chore like cleaning out and organizing your garage, for example? Even though every part of you wants to fight with the doing of the activity, you still get your shit together and clean out the garage. My experience of writing has sometimes felt just like that. I don't necessarily want to liken the writing of this book to cleaning out a garage, but on days where my energy has been low and my mind has not felt that exciting spark of interest, writing has in some way felt like a chore. However, I know that the contribution associated with the writing of this book is not at all like cleaning out a garage. It is actually a contribution that has excited me since the first words were being put to paper, even on the mentally and emotionally cloudy days.

IMAGINE YOU ARE STANDING, SITTING OR LYING down at the bottom of that figurative hole we were referring to earlier. During the course of reading this book, what has been the one thing that you know to be true about your contribution to the world? Is your contribution centered on being the best parent you can be? Are you looking to start your own business or embark upon a course of study that will bring you a new skill set so that you can get a better job and make more money? Perhaps like me, you are a forever student and are simply looking to consign even more delightful knowledge into the shelves of your mind. It doesn't matter how this contribution manifests. What matters is the identification and acknowledgment of the thing that gets you going in spite of what is happening externally or internally. When we are in full alignment with our best self, our purpose-fueled contribution can continue to flow outward from us.

My current sense of purpose and clarification of my contribution was extracted out of a dark night of the soul—I shared elements of that journey with you earlier in this book. I discovered that I wanted to be of service to others and made the determination that my most aligned way of being of service was to happen through my becoming a psychotherapist and coach. My personal experience with facing loss when I discovered my spouse had cheated provided the impetus to begin writing this book. Is this to say that we only discover our sense of purpose and contribution through adversity or difficult times? Not at all. It just so happens that my experiences, the difficult ones, have brought me clarity and focus each time they have occurred, kind of like a gentle spanking from the universe. Luminous moments where I have been acknowledged for a contribution I have made, perhaps a client expressing gratitude for the help I have provided, have also reinforced my certainty about walking a path that is in alignment with my life's purpose.

So, IN THIS VERY MOMENT, WHILE YOU ARE READING these words, take a pause. When was the last time you set your intention to get outside of yourself? Think about it. Was it today? Yesterday? Perhaps you can't remember. Perhaps you have been immersed in the suffering directly related to what we are exploring in this book and you haven't created space to gaze at yourself lovingly and take a moment to climb out of that misery. Ask yourself the questions, "When am I going to do the thing he is talking about here? When am I going to get outside of this suffering and engage in some activity that gets my mind away from the rumination on how 'bad' things are?"

PAUSE.

. . .

ASK THE QUESTIONS AGAIN.

IF YOU HAVE MANAGED TO DO THIS, THEN GUESS what? You just got outside of yourself long enough to create the space we were exploring earlier. If you can create that space for a few seconds, then you have the capacity to carry it forward into longer periods of time—a few minutes, hours or days. Real healing occurs when we spend time in the space we have so tenderly created to study ourselves.

WHAT ARE YOU WILLING TO DO TO GET OUTSIDE OF yourself? When you begin to notice that you are bogged down and colluding with the type of thinking that is keeping you out of forward momentum, what activity or thought process will you engage to climb out of that figurative hole?

I WILL REMIND YOU ONCE AGAIN OF YOUR wholeness and completeness and that the answers you seek reside within you.

AND ONWARD WE GO ...

17

Lighten Up

If we can't laugh at ourselves then what are we actually doing?

What can be said about taking a lighter approach or point of view as we walk down our path? Have you ever met someone who, even in moments of great conflict or struggle, has been able to keep a sense of humor or approach difficulty with a lightness of being while maintaining the integrity of who they really are? I marvel at people who do this with ease. My tendency is to get gritty and take everything just a little bit too seriously. It's not that I can't engage the lightness of being I am speaking to here, but it is not an effortless act. Touching a lighter quality of being requires me to pivot internally and make a conscious shift in my perception. It is kind of like putting on a different pair of lenses through which I am viewing the world around me. These lenses don't have to be rosy pink, but it is quite nice when they are not metaphorically smeared with mud and poop.

THE WEEK AFTER SIGNING DIVORCE PAPERS, I HAD the splendid experience of moving to Scotland for a period of time to live with my marvelously dynamic friend Maria and her equally dynamic spouse. Having just returned from Italy before spending a couple of weeks in America, settling in with friends for a longer stay was a welcome bit of respite, even if it was another moderately unfamiliar place. One thing I noticed right from the beginning was that the Scottish people seem to have a magnificent capacity for engaging life full on while not sweating the small stuff. It wasn't long after I arrived that I met another individual who, along with my friends, inspired me to write this chapter. With the mix of divorce, a good amount of international travel and having just dismantled a home alongside recon-necting with friends, all of this happening within a couple of weeks, it can be said that my system was experiencing some amount of sensory overload to say the least.

. . .

I HAD ONLY BEEN IN SCOTLAND FOR AROUND FIVE OR so days and was spending some time wandering the streets of Glasgow with a new friend. Feeling the tug between events of the recent past while holding the luminous prospects of the future in my mind and heart, I felt my system begin to feel a sense of overload. There was certainly not a lightness of being present within me—more like the swirl of an impending meltdown that eventually made its way out of my system and onto the pavement of a Glasgow street corner roiling unceremoniously between myself and my new friend. It felt like vomiting up a demonic presence straight out of some supernatural horror film—not pretty yet not entirely unwelcome since I have believed for a long time that allowing my vulnerability to show is the only way I want to be in this world. Even though vulnerability is a superpower, being vulnerable in the presence of others can sometimes be an uncomfortable experience … for them. It is in these moments that we must remind ourselves that just because someone is uncomfortable with our vulnerability, it does not mean that there is anything bad happening, nor is there anything wrong with us. They can take care of themselves during our moment of vulnerability and if they are not able to hold space with us, that inability has nothing to do with us.

. . .

THIS PERSON OF SCOTTISH DESCENT DID THEIR BEST to be present to my moment of suffering and in full alignment with their background, culture and upbringing; they reminded me that perhaps lightening up a bit might be called for in this instance. It was intended to be a helpful remark that later, with some greater clarity, I was able to reflect upon. I shifted to noticing how it was a lovely day, how we were on our way to have a fabulous lunch and how the overall experience of connection while exploring this dynamic city need not be bulldozed by a moment of suffering being born out of the tug between past and future. It was an uncomfortable moment for me since my monkey mind decided to bombard me with reasons why this person might not wish to spend any more time with me after this. Had I found real presence in that specific moment, my mind might have stayed out of that wretched fusion of the past and the future. The avalanche of discomfort I was experiencing might have been averted with a more mindful presence since nothing occurring in that specific moment was creating the suffering I was experiencing. The suffering engulfing me was solely related to the strain between everything but the present moment. When I arrived home that evening, I spoke briefly to my friends about some of the experience I was having and how I had been feeling a tug between past and future. The nutshell response from my friend Maria was "just go with the flow," to which her spouse wholeheartedly agreed. Both returned their attention to the TV program we were watching and that was the end of it. Simple. Genius. No biggie. I really needed to learn how to lighten up. To date, having been immersed in a culture that shrugs off adversity and gets moving without a second thought, I can state wholeheartedly that I am getting better at lightening up.

By now, I imagine you have become quite adept at noticing how your mind works in relation to every experience occurring on your life path. You, courageous reader, have been practicing mindful awareness using the tools we have discussed earlier in this book. So, how might you make a shift into a lighter way of being in moments when discomfort seems to be the heaviest element? Do you remember RAIN? If you have had any version of the story I just told you, then this would be the prime moment to engage the practice of recognizing, allowing and accepting, investigating and practicing non-identification. I'm sure you remember COAL. In this moment, you can allow yourself to become curious about, open to and accepting of everything in your current experience; these are some of the most loving ways of being that we as human beings can fully employ.

AND HERE WE ARE. ENOUGH SAID. I HAVE NO OTHER tools to present here that we haven't already observed together. So, lighten up when you need to.

IF I CAN DO IT, SO CAN YOU.

18

Follow Through

If you cannot gentle with yourself,
you may often find yourself stuck
between the proverbial rock and a hard place.

Here we are at the end of this little guidebook. Some of you may be questioning whether or not you can follow through with some of the tools and practices offered here, even if they sound helpful. Once again, I will remind you of your wholeness and completeness. You have your own answers and if you choose to trust that I am right about that, then you will connect with your ability to follow through and incorporate the lessons from this little book.

. . .

As always, be gentle and know that whatever pace you move through the loss you have experienced and however long you remain in uncertainty that this too shall pass. There is light nearer to you than you might imagine at all times, even when we feel as though we are surrounded by darkness. We have observed many tools and you possess countless that this book didn't explore because those tools are inherently yours. Remember to share what you have learned about yourself with others so that by passing along your wisdom, someone else's suffering will be diminished and you will have contributed to not only their well-being but to the well-being of everyone who crosses their path in the future. It is simply love, and nothing, not even the darkest of the dark, can stop that force. Love's true nature is to permeate everything and by setting your intention to carry love forward, you change the world for the better. You are that powerful.

Love and light to you!

Suggested Reading

The following list contains works by individuals who have inspired me on my life path. Without their wisdom, this book would not have been possible. I suggest reading everything on this list!

- Brené Brown - *Daring Greatly, Braving the Wilderness, Rising Strong*
- Joseph Campbell - *The Hero with a Thousand Faces, The Hero's Journey*
- Ram Dass - *Polishing the Mirror, Be Here Now*
- Pema Chödrön - *When Things fall Apart, Comfortable with Uncertainty, Start Where You Are, Welcoming the Unwelcome*
- Dawna Markova - *I Will Not Die an Unlived Life, No Enemies Within, Reconcilable Differences*

- Kemi Nekvapil - *The Gift of Asking*
- Eckhart Tolle - *The Power of Now, A New Earth, Stillness Speaks*
- Tara Brach - *Radical Acceptance, True Refuge, Radical Compassion*
- Daniel Siegel - *The Neurobiology of We, The Developing Mind, Mindsight,*
- Iyanla Vanzant - *In the Meantime, Get Over It!*
- Maria Nemeth - *The Energy of Money, Mastering Life's Energies*